Saint John Neumann

Saint John Neumann

Missionary to Immigrants

Written by Laura Rhoderica Brown, FSP
Illustrated by Virginia Esquinaldo

Pauline
BOOKS & MEDIA
Boston

Library of Congress Cataloging-in-Publication Data

Names: Brown, Laura Rhoderica, author. | Esquinaldo, Virginia, illustrator.
Title: Saint John Neumann : missionary to immigrants / written by Laura Rhoderica Brown, FSP ; illustrated by Virginia Esquinaldo.
Description: Boston, MA : Pauline Books & Media, 2016.
Identifiers: LCCN 2016021509| ISBN 9780819890665 (pbk.) | ISBN 0819890669 pbk.)
Subjects: LCSH: Neumann, John, Saint, 1811-1860--Juvenile literature. | Christian saints--United States--Biography--Juvenile literature.
Classification: LCC BX4700.N4 .B76 2016 | DDC 282.092 [B] --dc23
LC record available at https://lccn.loc.gov/2016021509

Cover art and illustrations by Virginia Esquinaldo

"P" and PAULINE are registered trademarks of the Daughters of Saint Paul.

Published by Pauline Books & Media, 50 Saint Paul's Avenue, Boston, MA 02130-3491

Printed in the U.S.A.

SJN VSAUSAPEOILL8-1610064 9066-9

www.pauline.org

Pauline Books & Media is the publishing house of the Daughters of Saint Paul, an international congregation of women religious serving the Church with the communications media.

1 2 3 4 5 6 7 8 9   20 19 18 17 16

Encounter the Saints Series

Blesseds Jacinta and Francisco Marto
Shepherds of Fatima

Blessed James Alberione
Media Apostle

Blessed Pier Giorgio Frassati
Journey to the Summit

Journeys with Mary
Apparitions of Our Lady

Saint Anthony of Padua
Fire and Light

Saint Andre Bessette
Miracles in Montreal

Saint Bernadette Soubirous
And Our Lady of Lourdes

Saint Catherine Labouré
And Our Lady of the Miraculous Medal

Saint Clare of Assisi
A Light for the World

Saint Elizabeth Ann Seton
Daughter of America

Saint Faustina Kowalska
Messenger of Mercy

Saint Francis of Assisi
Gentle Revolutionary

Saint Gianna Beretta Molla
The Gift of Life

Saint Ignatius of Loyola
For the Greater Glory of God

Saint Joan of Arc
God's Soldier

Saint John Paul II
Be Not Afraid

Saint Kateri Tekakwitha
Courageous Faith

Saint Martin de Porres
Humble Healer

Saint Maximilian Kolbe
Mary's Knight

Saint Pio of Pietrelcina
Rich in Love

Saint Teresa of Avila
Joyful in the Lord

Saint Thérèse of Lisieux
The Way of Love

Saint Thomas Aquinas
Missionary of Truth

Saint Thomas More
Courage, Conscience, and the King

*For even more titles in the
Encounter the Saints series,
visit: www.pauline.org./EncountertheSaints*

CONTENTS

1

GROWING IN GRACE

"Mama! Mamaaaaaaaa! I can hear John talking to himself. Tell him to go to sleep!"

"Wenceslaus, what is going on?" asked Mama Agnes as she shuffled into the boys' bedroom, yawning.

Her eldest son, John, still fully dressed, was sitting on his bed. The ten-year-old boy did not seem to notice his mother enter the room. He ran one hand through his tousled hair as his dark brown eyes were trained on the book he was intently reading. Her youngest son, Wenceslaus—or Wenzel as he was often called—rubbed his eyes from where he lay tucked in bed.

"Why in heaven's name are you not asleep, John Nepomucene (nay-POE-moo-seen) Neumann? Do you realize you're keeping Wenzel awake? You may be named after Bohemia's patron saint, Saint John of Nepomucene, but you're not being very nice to your little brother."

John looked up, startled at the sound of her voice. He smiled at her and said excitedly,

"Papa told me today about the day I was baptized. He said that because of my Baptism I can receive Jesus in the Eucharist tomorrow. I just thought I would read some more about Baptism before I go to bed."

John noticed his mother's eyebrows furrowing in frustration and added, "I'm sorry, Mama. I know it's late. I'm just excited to receive my first Communion tomorrow."

Mama Agnes' face softened. "I understand, John. Tomorrow is a special day . . . which is why you need to go to sleep. Besides, you already know that catechism backward and forward. That's why our parish priest said that you could receive your first Communion!"

"You're right, Mama. But I feel that no matter how much I learn, there is so much *more* to learn." John sighed. "Mama, I was just wondering what that day was like, when I was baptized. Who was there?"

"Yeah," Wenzel piped in. "I don't remember John being baptized. What was it like?"

Mama sighed and sat down on the bed. She thought for a moment and said, "It was March 28, 1811, the same day John was born. You weren't there, Wenzel, because you weren't born yet; neither were your sisters Joan or Louisa. And I wasn't there because I

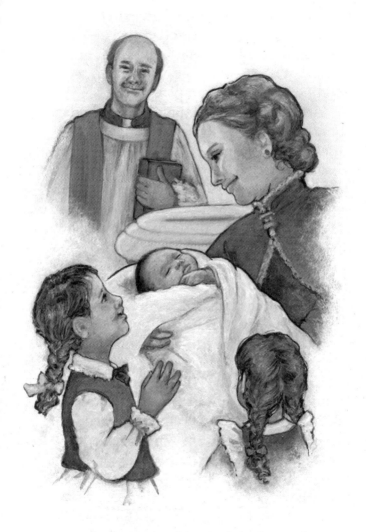

*"I don't remember John being baptized.
What was it like, Mama?"*

needed to rest. But John's godparents, the Mareks, and your sisters Catherine and Veronica were all present."

"I bet Catherine and Veronica were giggling the whole time," laughed John.

"Aren't they always giggling together about something?" Wenzel guffawed and jumped up on John's bed to listen more closely to Mama Agnes' story.

Mama Agnes paused for a moment and smiled. "Papa was so proud to have a son. He was smiling from ear to ear the entire day. He was so happy when both of you came into the world, just as he was when the girls were born."

Then with a faraway look in her eyes, she added, "And he was so happy to see you baptized, John. The workers in his weaving shop told me he was practically bursting with pride that day." She smoothed John's hair and then continued, "And I remember Papa told me that when Father baptized you, he said that he had a feeling that God had some amazing plans for your life." She smiled, then patted Wenzel on the head. "Which of course is true for you both."

John thought for a moment. "It is amazing, Mama, that God has a plan for everyone. And that he comes to live in our souls through Baptism and then he comes to us in the Eucharist! It's almost too much to understand. But I was wondering something. . . ."

"As you always do!" laughed Mama. "One last question, and then you must go to sleep; you have a big day tomorrow."

"Well, I was thinking about how Jesus is in heaven, but I will also receive him tomorrow! He will be in two places at the same time! How is that possible?"

"Yeah, Mama, how does he do that?" Wenzel, who had been falling asleep, sat up in his bed.

Mama Agnes smiled at them and said, "I suppose because he is God, so he is all-powerful and can be everywhere at all times. I remember during one homily our pastor said that God is not bound by time or space like we are."

"Oh, that makes sense," said John; then he added, "and, well, as I was thinking about heaven, I began to think about many things. I have so many questions!"

"Oh John, you are always full of questions. But it's late; you should be sleeping, not thinking!"

"But Mama, I have one last question! How is it that clouds float in the air without falling?"

"John, that's enough questions for one night. Let the clouds float; you don't have to hold them. You'll learn much more the more you go to school. You're a very intelligent boy. Look how well you've done in school so far." She stood up from the bed and kissed both boys on the forehead. "But right now, both of you go to sleep."

Early the next morning the Neumann family headed to the Church of St. James in their small village of Prachatitz (PRA-ha-jeets) in Bohemia. The church was decorated beautifully with many flowers on the altar, flowers that John's sisters had picked. Mama Agnes and Papa Philip were sitting in the pews with all of John's siblings. They all were dressed in their very best. John sat up in one of the first few pews, nervously twist-ing his hands together. He had prepared so long for this sacrament, and now it was actu-ally happening.

The Mass started as people were still coming through the doors; some even had to stand along the walls. When the choir sang the Gloria, John was filled with joy. He had begun going regularly to Mass with his mother, so he knew almost all of the parts of the Mass by heart. But on this special day he paid particular attention to every detail. When John saw the priest raise the Eucharist after the consecration, he thought, *Maybe one day I will be a priest and will be able to give the Body of Jesus to other people!*

After Mass, the townspeople gathered in the church hall to celebrate. John's mouth watered at the mountains of food: sauerkraut, sausages, beer for the grown-ups, and lots of sweets. They all enjoyed the music and dancing.

"What a special day, John! I hope you remember this day when you are older," Mama Agnes said proudly as they left the church.

"Oh, I will. I waited so long for it!" John exclaimed.

"You are growing up so quickly," Mama said. "Before you know it, you'll be leaving home to continue going to school."

"Away from home? When will that be?" John asked curiously.

"In a couple of years. . . . Your father and I think it would be good for you to go to school away from home."

Away from home . . . the words echoed in John's head. His heart sank.

2

LEAVING HOME

"I don't want you to go, John!" Wenceslaus cried with tear-filled eyes.

John spoke softly to his younger brother, "I know, Wenzel, but you can't come with me." John was now twelve years old and had been admitted to the Gymnasium in Budweis (BOOD-vise), a school for advanced students. Budweis was a day's journey from his family's village of Prachatitz. John was happy to continue studying, but it was going to be difficult to be away from his family.

"But why can't I go with you?" Wenzel exclaimed.

"Because you're too young," answered Catherine, John's oldest sister. "Now tell us where you put John's satchel. . . ."

"I know where he put it!" said Joan and Louisa, John's younger sisters, almost in unison.

Joan ran off and came back triumphantly holding the satchel. Wenzel's face crinkled in anger as he crossed his arms.

"I know you all will miss me, but I will be home for vacations and holidays," said John. "I promise!"

"Who says we will miss you, John?" teased Catherine with a smile. "I'm looking forward to not having to listen to your constant questions and reflections. You think too much!"

John laughed and gave Catherine a hug, then bent down to hug each of his siblings. *I will miss my family so much. Can I really do this?* John thought as his face grew serious. *Can I be away from the family I love so much?*

The sound of Papa Philip's voice broke through his thoughts. "Hurry up, John!" Papa Philip called out. "Time to go!"

"Yes, Papa. I'm coming," responded John.

Mama Agnes stood in the front doorway of the family's home. She looked at her eldest son and tried to smile.

"John," she said quietly in Czech. The Neumann family usually spoke German, so John knew to pay special attention when Mama Agnes spoke to him in her native language. "I know you'll study hard," she continued, "you always do. And don't feel too sad. We will miss each other, but it is because your family loves you so much that we miss you!"

"I'll miss all of you too, Mama. And yes, I'll study hard," John promised.

John's four sisters gathered at the door with Mama Agnes and Wenzel as John walked down the front path toward the wagon. Sitting next to his father, John turned and waved even as he fought back tears. Papa Philip guided the horses down the road.

John sat quietly and watched as they passed the places he knew so well. "Papa," John wondered aloud, "what do you think this school will be like?"

"You will have good teachers and you will share a room with some other boys. Are you feeling nervous, John?" Papa said gently. After a moment of silence, Papa Philip continued, "It's normal to feel nervous. Don't be embarrassed. It's hard to be away from family. But I think this will be good for you. You'll learn so much at the Gymnasium in Budweis. You love to learn, John; it is a gift."

"It's true, Papa," said John. "I hate to leave all of you, but I am excited to study. I can't wait to learn more. I especially want to learn more languages; I loved studying Latin in Prachatitz. And I want to learn more about botany and astronomy. There is just so much to learn!"

Papa Philip laughed. "That's my boy! See, you will come back with a head full of knowledge; very soon you will know more than I."

"I doubt that, Papa. You read so much!" laughed John.

"I will miss our evenings reading by the fire, son," said Papa.

"Me too," said John sadly.

"But son, you will make some good friends, and before you know it, you will feel right at home," said Papa Philip reassuringly.

"I hope so," said John a little doubtfully.

"Let's say a prayer to your patron saint, and the patron saint of Bohemia. He'll help you," said Papa Philip brightly. "Saint John Nepomucene, please pray for my son John during this transition in going to school away from family. Help him to stay close to Jesus and to confide in him when he faces difficulty, and help him to always find strength in his faith."

John raised his head and looked intently at his father. "Thank you, Papa." His heart felt more peaceful. But John could still feel his stomach churning.

I hope I find good friends in Budweis, thought John.

3

Meeting Adalbert

"Hey, little man, think you're smart, don't you?" yelled Hubert, one of John's classmates. "Well, your smarts won't help you grow another few inches, shorty!" Hubert walked toward John and shoved him against the wall.

"Hey, that's enough!" A tall boy came between John and his classmate and separated them. The tall boy grabbed John by the elbow and they headed outside.

"Don't you worry, John. Hubert is always like that. I think he was born angry," said the boy as they walked. "Plus, he is just jealous of you. I think we all are; you *are* pretty smart!"

John smiled gratefully at the boy. "Thanks for helping me out. What is your name?"

"Adalbert Schmidt."

"Adalbert, it's nice to meet you. We should take a walk sometime or maybe study together!"

Adalbert was right. John did not have any problem with his studies. John's old teacher had prepared the boys from Prachatitz well for the Gymnasium. In fact, he had prepared them so well that they already knew much of the material.

Well, I don't need to study that much, because I already know a lot of this stuff. Since I have all this extra time on my hands, what shall I do? John thought. *I know: I'll read! I'll go to the school's library and see what books they have!*

"I really like the library books on the natural sciences," he told Adalbert one day. "They are fascinating, especially this one on botany. I love learning the names of all of the plants and flowers that I've known by sight for so long."

"Yes," agreed Adalbert. "I enjoy learning about plants too. I love all types of science!"

"And I am so happy to learn more languages. I'm excited that we'll learn Greek. I have loved speaking different languages ever since I learned German and Czech growing up," said John.

"Well, you are alone there. I don't really like languages like you do, John," Adalbert laughed.

John's first years at the school went smoothly, but when he was fifteen years old and in his fourth year at the Gymnasium, trouble struck.

"Our religion teacher is so boring, I can hardly stand it," John complained one day to Adalbert. "I can barely stay awake in his class!"

Adalbert nodded in agreement. Then he added, "And the Latin professor is terrible too. Most days he comes to class drunk! How can they expect us to learn anything?!"

The Latin teacher was finally fired and a new teacher took his place. But the change came too late. The students were so far behind in their studies that no one, including John, could keep up with all the new work they were given.

"Too much homework! Our new teacher must be crazy!" John overheard one boy complaining as a group of students trudged down the school corridor. "How can he expect us to do all of this work? Does he know what he is asking of us?" John silently agreed.

At the end of a difficult school year, the boys from Prachatiz gathered together on the front steps waiting to head home. Some of the boys had failed their courses.

"I am so glad this year is over," one boy yelled as he threw his report card into the air. "I've had enough of this. No more school for me!"

Others chimed in: "No more school for me either!"

"Hey, Neumann, let me see your report card," said Hubert. "I bet you didn't do so well for once."

It was true. John had not done well. His grades were only slightly above failing, and he was ashamed of himself. He hung his head, not responding to Hubert's taunts. *I don't know what to do!* John thought. *I'll have to show my report card to my parents sooner or later. Should I quit too?*

Adalbert moved close to John; he seemed to know what his good friend was thinking.

"What's wrong with you, Neumann?" Adalbert whispered.

John remained silent for a moment and then said quietly, "I feel so discouraged, Adalbert. And my parents will be so disappointed. Is it even worth it to continue? I've never done so poorly."

"But you can't quit, John. You've got the brains! And besides, the good Lord would not like it one bit!"

John appreciated Adalbert's encouragement, but he felt unsure. Just then, John spotted Papa Philip driving up in the family wagon.

"Don't forget what I said!" called Adalbert as John headed down the school steps. "And don't lose hope. You are meant for great things!"

On the way home John was lost in his thoughts. Thankfully, Papa Philip did not ask about his report card. But John knew he could not hide it forever, and the very thought of what his parents would say made his stomach ache.

"My bookworm doesn't want to go to school?"

4

TROUBLE AT HOME

"What's wrong, John? Did something go wrong at school?"

John didn't know what to say. He had been home for an entire week, but he hadn't said a word about his grades.

"I can tell that you're happy to be home," Mama Agnes continued, "but I know something is bothering you. Please tell me."

John looked at his mother and sighed deeply. "I have some bad news." He took a deep breath and then blurted out, "My grades were bad this year. Maybe I should quit school."

"My bookworm doesn't want to go to school?" Mama Agnes said with surprise. "You've always received good grades. . . . It can't be that bad," she said as she reached out to hug him. "Let's go sit under the apple tree in the yard. Then you can tell me what happened."

John was relieved to tell his mother about his disastrous year.

Mama Agnes listened carefully to him and then said, "John, I could tell from your letters that something was wrong, but I wish you had confided in your father and me earlier. It sounds like you had a bad teacher. We will have to pray about what to do now."

That evening as the family finished supper, Papa Philip turned to John and said, "Your mother tells me you had some problems this year at school. You haven't shown me your grades, son. Where are they?"

John's heart began to pound and his face flushed red. "My report card is up in my room, Papa," John replied as he rose slowly from the table to retrieve it. *Now I'm really afraid; what will Papa say?* John thought.

Returning to the table, John handed his father his grades. Papa Philip pulled out his glasses and put them on. His eyes widened in surprise. "You are a bright, studious boy, John. Why such poor grades?"

"One of my teachers had a drinking problem, so he did not teach us very well. But when he left, the teacher who replaced him was so difficult. I could not keep up!" Then John added, "And it was also hard for me to concentrate because I was sharing a room with other boys who were not serious about their work."

Papa Philip raised his eyebrows. "John," he said with disappointment in his voice, "you know a shared room was all that we could afford. You seem to be blaming everyone but yourself. Beginning tomorrow, you will stay home and work for me in the weaving shop. You need some time to think about what you want to do with your life."

John nodded sadly. When Papa Philip spoke with that tone, John knew there was no changing his father's mind.

The next day and each morning for many weeks, John reported promptly at eight o'clock to work in his father's weaving shop.

I should have told Papa about my troubles in school before I had to bring a bad report card home, John thought bitterly. *He may have been more open to hearing my explanation.*

John was not happy working in the weaving shop, but it did give him time to think and to pray as his father had suggested.

Please, Jesus, help me know what I should do. Should I just accept that I am not meant to continue studying?

One day as John was working in the weaving shop, Papa Philip came in and stood near him.

"I've been meaning to tell you that you're doing very well here. You learn quickly. I'm proud of you, son. One day the shop will be yours."

John looked up at Papa Philip and said tentatively, "I've been praying like you suggested, Papa, and I don't think I want to be a weaver. I want to go back to school."

"But John, your grades were so poor."

"I know, Papa. I understand. I had some difficult obstacles last year, but I think I also took school for granted. I promise I'll try harder if you send me back, Papa," John pleaded. Then after a pause, he added, "Plus, Mama thinks I should have another chance."

"I see I am outnumbered! Yes, your mother and I have been talking about this," said Papa Philip with a smile. "But," he added, "I still don't feel sure it makes sense."

Suddenly John had an idea. "Papa, Father Meyer from the Gymnasium is here in Prachatitz staying with the Smutneys. You could ask him to give me a test to see if I am prepared to continue."

Papa Philip thought for a moment. "But a test does not prove you have the motivation to do well, John. Do you have what it takes?"

"Papa, I have to study hard for this test. If I don't pass with flying colors, then you will know that I am not motivated."

Papa Philip nodded. "Fine. If you do really well on the test, I'll consider allowing you to return to school."

John beamed.

On the feast of Saint Wenceslaus, a Bohemian prince who was martyred, the weaving shop was closed. The Neumann family gathered in their backyard to relax under the apple trees.

Just then Wenzel came walking quickly down the garden path. "Papa," he said excitedly, "a man at the front gate is asking for you!"

"Well then, show him in, son," Papa Philip responded.

Moments later, Father Meyer came into the backyard.

"Pleased to meet you, Mr. Neumann," he said as he extended his hand in greeting.

"I have known your son John for some time and have been very impressed. He's a bright boy and is especially good with languages."

John's heart was beating fiercely as he looked down at the two men from the tree he'd been climbing. John had studied hard before he took the test, but he was not sure how well he had done. He supposed he was about to find out. John jumped down from the tree onto the grass beside Father Meyer.

The priest placed his hand on John's shoulder. "Mr. Neumann, I'm happy to report that your son has done remarkably well on the examination!"

Mama Agnes' face lit up with delight. "I knew John could do it!"

"Sir, it would be a shame to waste such a fine mind. Won't you consider allowing John to go back to school?" Father Meyer added.

John's heart began to beat more wildly. *Would Papa allow him to go back to school?*

Papa Philip smiled. "If you think he can succeed and John is sure he wants to continue studying, I am willing to give it a second chance."

John grinned. "I am sure, Papa! Thank you!"

5

DOCTOR OR PRIEST?

"I can't believe we have graduated," said Adalbert. "And you with honors!" he added as he slapped John on his back.

The sun shone brightly as Adalbert and John rode in an open coach on their way home to Prachatitz. It was early June 1831, and John was now twenty years old. John had kept his word. He had studied hard and had done very well in his studies. John was thankful that Papa Philip had found a way to pay for him to have his own room. This had helped him to concentrate and do well in his classes.

"But now we have to decide what we're going to do next," said John, feeling nervous.

Adalbert's face grew serious. "I know you pray every day, John, and read spiritual books. But have you decided on your vocation? How will you best serve God? What does God want you to do?"

John responded hesitantly, "I have felt drawn to both the priesthood and medicine for a long time. But I don't know for sure if

God is calling me to be a priest. Why would he call *me* anyway? And even if he were, I'd *like* to go to the seminary, but it's difficult to get in. I would need recommendations from important people."

"John, you get discouraged too easily! And you think too little of yourself. I would not be surprised at all if God called you," responded Adalbert. "As for me, I think God is calling me to be a priest, so I'm going to apply to the seminary!"

As they neared Prachatitz, the coach slowed down to let the boys off.

"Let's get together this summer!" said Adalbert. The two young men waved as they parted ways, heading to their homes.

When John arrived at the front gate of his house, he found Wenzel waiting for him.

"It's great to see you, little brother," John said as he hugged Wenzel. "Hey, you aren't so little anymore, are you?" John looked his brother up and down. "What has Mama been feeding you?" he joked.

"You'll see soon enough!" replied Wenzel with a smile. Just then the front door flew open. Mama Agnes ran out wearing a bright blue kitchen apron with her hair pulled back in a bun.

"John!" she called as she opened her arms to embrace him. "You're just in time for supper. We've prepared something special for you: *veprove se zelim* (veh-pro-VEH / seh / zeh-LEEM) your favorite!"

Following his mother and brother inside, John silently prayed, *Thank you, God, for my wonderful family. It feels so good to be home.*

John took his friend's advice and spent time praying about his future. He knew his parents would soon ask him about his plans and he needed to ask God for guidance. Every morning, he accompanied Mama Agnes to daily Mass and spent time in prayer.

God, please make it clear to me what you want for my life.

One night after dinner, Papa Philip turned to John and Mama Agnes. "Let's move into the parlor to talk."

Papa Philip reached for his pipe and sat in his big chair by the fireplace. Turning to his son he said, "You've done *very* well in school, son. I am glad we decided to send you back. I am proud of you," Papa concluded as he looked over John's grades.

"Now what will you do with this knowledge?" said Mama Agnes.

"Son, I know you've been interested in becoming a doctor, and that would require further study. You need to decide if you are going to continue studying, because the universities open soon." Papa Philip looked straight at John and continued, "And what about the priesthood; have you felt like God might be calling you to be a priest?"

John looked at his mother. Mama Agnes did not say anything, but John had the feeling that she would love to see him enter the priesthood. John thought, *It's true that I've thought about becoming a priest, but why should I try? I won't be accepted into the seminary.*

"No matter what you choose, your mother and I are proud of you," said Papa Philip.

After a long pause, John said, "Can I think and pray about it, Papa? I have been praying, but I think I need more time."

"Of course, son, we will pray that God leads you to the right decision," said Papa Philip.

Everyone in the Neumann family went to bed early that night—everyone except John. He couldn't sleep, so he stayed up reading by candlelight. Late in the night, John heard a soft knock on his door.

"John, can I come in?" Mama Agnes asked softly as she opened the door.

At John's nod she entered carrying a lighted candle. She sat down on the edge of John's bed and said, "I noticed the light in your room. Can't sleep?"

He looked shyly at his mother. "Not really. I'm confused, Mama."

"Is this about our conversation this evening?"

John decided to ask the question that pestered him. "Do you or Papa have influential friends in Budweis or Prague?"

"Why do you ask, John?" Mama Agnes asked, puzzled.

"Did you know that to get into the Seminary of Budweis I need an important sponsor? I don't know anyone like that. I'd never be accepted!"

Mama Agnes said excitedly, "So, you *do* want to become a priest!"

"Yes, Mama. I've been praying and I feel that God is calling me to be a priest. But I'm not sure it's possible."

"John, if God is calling you to become a priest, he will make a way," said Mama Agnes. "I want you to think about writing a letter, your very best, to the seminary in Budweis."

The next morning John went to the near-by church and prayed a long time.

Dear God, I feel a desire to become a priest and I think you may be calling me. Yet I am scared that if I try to apply to seminary and am rejected, I will be so disappointed! But I am going to trust in you. If this is your will, you will clear the way.

When John returned home he wrote a letter requesting entrance to the seminary. He waited anxiously for a response for two long weeks.

Then, one night, just as John was wondering why he hadn't yet received an answer, he heard a loud knock on the front door.

6

ROAD TO PRIESTHOOD

"John, a letter arrived for you!" Catherine called as she entered the dining room while curiously inspecting an envelope. John looked up, his heart beating wildly. *Did they accept me?* he wondered. He had told no one about his request to enter seminary—except his mother.

Handing him the letter, Catherine looked at her brother expectantly. "Hurry up and open it! It looks important!"

"I need some privacy," John replied apprehensively. He took the letter, jumped up from the table, and went to a side desk. With his father's long, silver letter opener, John quickly slit open the envelope and removed the piece of paper. Taking a deep breath, John unfolded the letter and began to read, his serious face gradually breaking into a smile.

"It must be good news, John," said Papa Philip, seeing his son's face light up with joy. "May I see?"

"Yes, Papa! Could you read it aloud?"

Papa Philip cleared his throat and began to read:

Dear Mr. John N. Neumann,

Your letter of application to the diocesan seminary in Budweis has been received and reviewed. After consultation, we have agreed to accept your application for admission. Please contact Father John Koerner, the Dean of the Seminary, for further instructions.

May God bless you,
Ernest Rudzicka,
Bishop of Budweis

Papa Philip paused for a few moments after he finished reading the letter. "I didn't know you would go ahead with such plans without telling me, son," he said with a grave face. Then he smiled and added, "But this is a great surprise; it's not every day that a man's son decides to become a priest! I fully support your decision!"

Veronica began to cheer. Wenzel placed two fingers in his mouth and let out a loud, shrill whistle. The whole family took turns hugging John.

Mama Agnes whispered in John's ear, "See, we have such a good God. When we pray, he hears! And he doesn't need important recommendations. If he wants you to become a priest, he makes a way."

Several weeks later, on November 1, 1831—All Saints' Day—Papa Philip dropped John off at the seminary entrance. As they rode along under blue skies on that crisp autumn day, Papa Philip told John, "If you are going to become a priest, be the best priest you can be! Give God your all!" Then he put his arm around John and drew him in for a brief hug.

"Thank you, Papa," John responded. "I'm going to miss you and the whole family so much, even though I am excited to start my studies."

One day, after registering for theology classes, John was walking down the steps when a familiar voice called out, "Hey, is that you Neumann?" John turned and saw Adalbert bounding down the seminary steps.

"Boy, am I glad to see you, John!" Adalbert said, coming closer and grabbing John's hand. "I knew you'd be accepted!"

John smiled and said, "And I am happy to see you!" They were both grateful to have a good friend as they started their seminary life.

John dove into his studies with vigor and purpose, and prayed with a new intensity. He still enjoyed the natural sciences, but not as much as before. Theology was now his passion. John knew that to prepare for the priesthood, he had to study theology and grow in prayer. More than anything else, he wanted to be a good and holy priest.

One afternoon as he and Adalbert were out walking by the Moldau River, not far from the seminary, John said, "Adalbert, I'm really enjoying theology. It's not at all like it was in the Gymnasium. Remember that boring religion professor we had there?"

"Do I ever!" said Adalbert, rolling his eyes and grinning. "I could barely stay awake during class!"

"Isn't Father Koerner's class on the Letters of Saint Paul amazing?" continued John. "He can really teach."

"Yes, he's fantastic," agreed Adalbert. "His class makes me want to become a missionary just like Saint Paul!"

"I've thought about that too, Adalbert," John responded. "Wouldn't it be exciting to travel to another country to tell others about God?"

From then on their desire to become missionaries grew stronger. They often went on walks and talked about their classes and what it would be like to be a priest in North America. They kept their hope secret, and only told a few people.

One day John said to Adalbert, "Did you know that most of the Catholic immigrants in North America speak German, French, and English? We already know German but we'll need to learn French and English, too, in order to help them."

"Well, John, you're great with languages so that shouldn't be a problem for you. You already speak German, Czech, Italian, Greek, Latin. . . . I've lost count!" said Adalbert.

"We can help each other; let's try to study French on our own," said John.

And so they began to study French and to practice speaking it on their walks. But English was much harder.

"How will we ever learn English?" asked Adalbert. "No one in Budweis speaks it."

John bowed his head and thought for a moment. "Trust in God, Adalbert, he will provide. You're usually the one telling *me* to have courage!" John and Adalbert laughed.

"I have an idea," John said suddenly. "I heard that English courses are taught at the

University of Prague. It's not far from the seminary there."

Adalbert looked excited as the idea dawned on him. "Bishop Rudzicka (roo-JHEET-ska) sends two seminarians each year to Prague. So, we could transfer to the seminary in Prague and learn English at the university!"

They began to eagerly discuss their plan to transfer to the seminary of Prague. Little did they know that things would not go as they planned.

7

ADVENTURES IN PRAGUE

"Anton Laad? How could he be chosen to go to Prague over you?!" John wailed.

Adalbert hung his head and said, "Well, at least the bishop chose you to go. I'll just have to learn English and continue to study French here in Budweis."

The next two years in Prague were difficult for John; he had never felt so lonely. He met other seminarians in Prague but still missed his family and Adalbert, his best friend. John shared all of this with Jesus, spending much time in prayer and writing in his journal.

How could I get through this without you, Jesus? The priests and seminarians here are very kind, but I still feel so alone. John paused for a moment in his prayer and looked up at the tabernacle, realizing he was wrong. *But I am never really alone. I have you, Jesus!*

John's language studies were another challenge. French was not taught at the seminary, and that year the seminarians were not allowed to take any classes at the

University of Prague. John thought forlornly, *My reason for transferring was completely useless! I might as well go back to Budweis.* But John knew he was just feeling homesick. He had decided to come here so he would have to make the best of it. *Jesus, I trust that you have a plan for me here. I am lonely, but maybe this will just give me lots of time to study the languages I need to learn!*

John studied French on his own and at the end of the year, when he asked to take the exam, he passed with flying colors!

But John found English more difficult than French, so he knew he needed help. One day when John was out taking a walk, he met a factory worker named Owens, from England. Owens invited him to come to his factory during break time. Owens and his friends would help John with his English. John was elated and met with the men a week later.

"Okay, John, here's what we will do," Owens said with a smile. "You tell us in English what you did this morning. We will correct your pronunciation and your grammar."

John cleared his throat and took a deep breath. "It's a deal," John replied, smiling broadly. He liked these simple, straightforward men. "But please, don't be too hard on me, especially with my pronunciation. Remember you are in Bohemia, not England!"

The men laughed loudly. They were happy to help this determined young man learn English, their language!

It was now June 1835 and John was excited because he had almost finished his studies. One day a letter arrived and he picked it up, frowning. It was from the bishop! What could it mean? His stomach churned a little as he opened it. Then he cried out, "What? But I have waited for so long!" The letter said that ordination was being postponed that year because the bishop had fallen ill. Besides that, the diocese already had a lot of priests, and the bishop felt it was not urgent to ordain more just then.

John put down the letter sadly and thought, *Why did you allow this to happen to me, Lord? I have studied so much and have been preparing for years. Now this?*

John put his hands over his face and prayed aloud, "Jesus, I know that you will help me through this. You have led me this far and will not leave me now. I trust you."

A feeling of peace began to fill John's heart as he prayed. He remembered his unexpected acceptance to the seminary in Budweis. He hadn't had recommendations from important people, only his handwritten letter. He felt certain that if Jesus wanted him to become a priest to serve his people in the United States, then Jesus would provide the way. John thought, *The idea of entering a religious community of priests has come to me from time to time. But it didn't seem like God was drawing me there. But now I'm starting to wonder . . .*

John took a stagecoach home to Prachatitz in July 1835. He was so happy to leave Prague since it had been so difficult there. Though he looked forward to spending time at home with his family, he also felt some anxiety. He hadn't yet told them about his plans to go to the United States, since he wasn't sure if it would happen. But he had to tell them soon.

One evening several weeks later, John broke the news to his family.

"I have something to tell all of you," John said, looking pensively at his mother and father and then slowly around the room at his siblings. John cleared his throat and continued, "First, I'd like you all to know how much I love you. God has truly blessed me in giving me such a loving family. . . ." For a moment he couldn't go on. Then he said, "I have something important to tell you that isn't easy to say . . . or hear." John knew he would miss them terribly and his heart was breaking. Taking a deep breath, he continued, "I feel that God is calling me to become a missionary priest in the United States."

His sisters gasped.

John continued, "I've been praying about this for over two years now, and I'm convinced that it is the Lord's will for me."

"But the United States is so far away!" Veronica cried out.

"Yes, but the immigrants greatly need priests," he replied. "They need priests to care for them who can speak their language."

He turned toward his mother. Their eyes met. She was very peaceful and serene.

"John, you're very generous and self-sacrificing. I'm so proud of you," said Mama Agnes, even as tears came to her eyes. "Going to the United States will be very difficult." She rose and gave John a hug as she said, "But when the good Lord asks something of us, he always gives the grace and strength to do it. He never leaves us alone. Go with my blessing, son."

Papa Philip had been silent while Mama Agnes talked. John thought he could see the glimmer of a tear in his father's eye.

Then Papa Philip said, "Although it pains me to see you go, I give you my blessing. We will miss you very much, John, but if this is God's will then we support you completely."

The only uncertainty that remained was the question of his ordination. They needed *priests* in the United States, not seminarians! With ordinations in his diocese postponed indefinitely, John thought, *How long will I need to wait? Will I have to travel to the United States before being ordained a priest? If I leave for the United States without a promise from a bishop to ordain me, I might risk never being ordained.*

The very thought terrified him!

8

OFF TO BE A MISSIONARY!

"Adalbert, have you heard that the ordinations have been postponed? Who knows when we will be ordained!"

"I guess we just have to be patient," Adalbert said.

"But Adalbert, we have been patient," John said. "It has been seven months and still no ordinations. How much longer can we possibly wait? We are wasting valuable time. The people in the United States greatly need priests! I feel that God is calling me to be a missionary now, not later!"

Adalbert looked surprised at John's intensity. Then John grew even more serious and said, "Adalbert, I've thought and prayed about this for some time. I'm going to the United States now. If God wants me to be ordained, then I will be ordained there. Will you come with me?"

Unable to face his friend, Adalbert looked down. "I've been thinking about it, too, but it's just too risky. We don't know if any

American bishop will welcome us. I just can't go without knowing that for sure."

John's face fell but he said sadly, "I understand how you feel and you're being prudent. But I must go. I keep thinking about the immigrants in the United States who are falling away from the Church because they have no priests. I trust that God will provide a way for me and he will see that I am ordained there."

"John, let's pray for each other and trust that our good Lord will take care of us," Adalbert said with a trembling voice.

With excitement but also a heavy heart, John prepared for the long and possibly dangerous journey by ship. He received his passport and had a small amount of money for travel. He knew that if he left for the United States, he might never return to his home. *Will I see my family again?* he often thought. *Only God knows the answer.*

"God, my Father," he prayed one night in his room, "I ask you for the courage to trust you and your Divine Providence. I will go to the United States, and if it is your will then I know that somehow I will be ordained a priest there after I arrive. I feel afraid but I trust you."

After John made his preparations, he began to think about how he would leave home. *Saying goodbye to Mama, Papa, and my sisters and brother is going to be very hard! Should I tell them that I'm going to leave without ordination? That would make it doubly painful . . .* Suddenly a thought came to him, *I'll tell my family I'm going to Budweis and I won't even mention the United States. I'll write them a letter after I leave.*

The next morning John rose early. He grabbed a piece of bread and his satchel and quietly slipped out of the house. He was off to Budweis. After reaching the city, he wrote his parents a letter.

Feb. 11, 1836

Dear Mama and Papa,

You must be wondering why I suddenly left home, and you deserve an explanation. I did it because I thought it would be less painful for you. I also know that saying goodbye to you and not knowing when I would see you again would be almost impossible for me to bear.

For three years I've been preparing to go to the United States. I want to serve God's people as a priest there. I had hoped that you would see me ordained and that you would be with me as I celebrate my first Mass. But this must not be God's will. However, someday, God willing, you will join me around the altar.

In a few days I will stop in Einsiedeln (INE-zee-diln) on my way to Strasbourg. There I will see a professor who might be able to help me connect with a bishop in the United States. I'll write again from Einsiedeln. I love you more than you know. Please tell Catherine, Veronica, Joan, Louise, and Wenzel that I love them, too.

Please pray for me.
Your devoted son,
John

While he was in Budweis, John went to see Bishop Rudzicka. He needed to receive his bishop's blessing before crossing the Atlantic Ocean.

"This is a risky undertaking, John," the bishop told him.

"Yes, I know, Bishop Rudzicka, but I feel it is God's will," said John. Then he slyly added, "Unless you are planning on holding the ordination tomorrow!"

The bishop laughed heartily, "No, John, I'm recovering from my illness, but we have plenty of priests right now. So I'm not planning on ordaining any seminarians for a while longer. But I give you my blessing. Go with God! I pray you will be ordained in the United States."

John breathed a sigh of relief as he bowed his head to receive the bishop's blessing.

John left and walked toward the center of Budweis where he found a stagecoach waiting. *This is it. I am actually doing this*, he thought. *I have prepared for so long, and now I am beginning this momentous journey.* Despite his anxiety, he boarded the stagecoach. Adalbert had joined him and they traveled together to Einsiedeln. After his friend left him there, a pang of loneliness came over John. He already missed his family and friends, especially Adalbert. *All those years of planning and dreaming together*, he thought. *They were wonderful times. Jesus, please take care of Adalbert and comfort my family. I am sure they miss me just as much as I miss them!*

John arrived in Strasbourg in late February, and he was warmly welcomed at the seminary. One of the professors, Canon Rass, kindly offered to write him a letter asking Bishop Dubois to admit John to the Diocese of New York.

While in Strasbourg, John was told of a generous merchant in Paris who might be able to finance his trip to the United States.

So John asked the professor to inform Bishop Dubois in his letter that John would wait in Paris for his response. Then the young man set off for Paris, feeling nervous.

But when John arrived in Paris he didn't find the generous merchant. And he grew increasingly worried as several more weeks passed and no letter arrived from Bishop Dubois. John was two hundred miles away from home, with little money and no promise of any financial help. He knew that he either needed to return home or continue with his plans, trusting in God.

9

HEADING TO A NEW LAND

While he was waiting in Paris, John prayed a lot and finally made the risky decision to press on for New York. He found a stagecoach and traveled with several other people to the coastal city of Le Havre, France. As they rode along he thought, *I hope I find a boat willing to take me to the United States for the little money I have left in my pocket. Will I have enough for my trip? Will I have enough to eat?*

His thoughts abruptly ended as the stagecoach slowed to a stop. John peered out the side window. He saw a small country inn nestled on the side of the road. An inviting sign read: "Food and Drink."

"I'm starving," said the gentleman sitting directly across from John. "Thank goodness we finally stopped to eat!"

John felt the small amount of change in his pocket as he followed the other passengers into the inn. *Jesus, I know I need to save all this money to help pay for my passage on the ship,* he prayed, *but I'm so very hungry. Jesus, provide for me!*

A woman motioned to John. *She must be the innkeeper's wife,* he thought. "Come here and sit down, young man," the woman said. "You look like you could use a good meal!"

John sat down reluctantly. *Will I have enough to pay?* he wondered.

"Where are you headed?" the woman asked with a hint of curiosity.

"I hope to go to the United States as a missionary. I want to serve God's people there as a priest!"

"How very courageous and generous," the woman said. "You'll need your strength and health for such a long journey." She paused a minute, noticing his frugal appearance. Then she added, "Your meal is on the house. All I ask is that you pray for us!"

John promised his prayers and left with a full stomach and a grateful heart. *Thank you, Jesus, for taking care of me!* he prayed as he rode on in the stagecoach.

As soon as they reached Le Havre, John walked straight to the dock where he saw the ocean for the first time in his life. The roaring waves breaking on the land took his breath away. Salty air blew across his face as he stood there, taking it all in. He praised and thanked God for this limitless expanse of churning water. *Thank you, Jesus, for this beautiful view and the wonder of your creation! I praise you, Lord!*

Afterward John began to look for a ship that would take him across the ocean. He was feeling nervous since he realized he didn't have much money. He approached the captain of one anchored ship. "Are any ships leaving for the United States soon?" Despite his fear, John's eyes shone brightly with excitement.

"Yes, this ship will leave in a few days," a man said gruffly, barely looking at him.

"Are you the captain?" said John tentatively. "I'd like to buy passage."

"We don't have room," the captain replied, as he turned away without another glance at John.

As John stood there, a wave of anxiety washed over him. If he couldn't find a boat in the next few days, he would have to turn back home.

Suddenly John saw a man standing next to a boat with the name *Europa* emblazoned on its side. Approaching him, John said, "Sir, are you the captain? I want to buy passage to the United States. I am a seminarian and I hope to be a missionary priest."

"Are any ships leaving for the United States soon?"

The captain looked down at John with slight interest. "Yes, I'm Captain Drummond. One hundred and twenty francs."

"Is that the lowest fare available, sir?" John asked with a gulp. He wanted to spend as little money as possible. He didn't know what awaited him in New York.

Captain Drummond's face relaxed, and he smiled slightly. "The lowest fare is ninety francs. But I will take eighty francs if you promise to pray that we have a safe trip."

John readily agreed. "Thank you, Captain. Thank you very much." His dream was coming true; he would soon be bound for the United States!

A few days later, John boarded the *Europa*, finally headed to the port of New York. *I'll have to be ordained once I arrive, but at least I'll have crossed this immense ocean!* John thought excitedly.

Spotting a space at the far end of the deck, John hurried toward it. Putting down his satchel, he gazed out on the wide ocean waters. *This is a good spot. I can watch the waves here, and pray. . . . The water is limitless, just like the goodness and providence of God!*

After six weeks at sea, the passengers could finally see land! But the captain of the *Europa* wanted to wait a few days before going into port, due to some sick passengers and heavy winds and rain. John begged to be let off the ship, and finally the captain allowed him to get into a rowboat bound for Staten Island. From there John took the small steamer *Hercules* and arrived in New York City. He had made it to the United States! It was Thursday, June 2, 1836—the feast of *Corpus Christi*, honoring the Body and Blood of Jesus.

John wanted to go to Mass and thank God for bringing him safely across the ocean. As he walked from the docks into the city, he saw many churches, but none of them were Catholic. John trudged up and down the streets of New York in the drizzling rain.

"There must be a Catholic church somewhere in this city!" he mumbled to himself.

Night was quickly setting in, and darkness filled the narrow streets. John's coat and clothing were soaking wet, and water oozed through the holes in his shoes. He was hungry and tired. Putting his hand in his pocket, John felt the few coins he had left and anxiously wondered, *What am I going to do now, Jesus?*

10

Answered Prayers

I can't go any farther right now, John thought. *I'll find a church tomorrow when I'm rested.*

John spotted an inn on a side street. He went in and was happy to find that the Swiss innkeeper spoke German. *It's good to hear my native language,* John thought, *even though I'll soon be putting my English skills to the test. But for now, sleep!* John took the key and headed straight to his room. Exhausted, he fell right to sleep.

The next day, the sun shone brightly through his window. Getting up, John knelt by the bed to pray. *Thank you, Lord, for a comfortable bed and a good night's sleep. It was so much better than the hard plank bed on the ship!*

John emptied his pockets on the dresser in his room. With just a few coins left, he would soon run out of money. *Well, I hope I'll soon find someone who can help me,* he thought. His stomach rumbled with hunger and anxiety. John went downstairs, put his last coins on the front desk, and asked the innkeeper for some breakfast. The man plopped a big, steaming bowl of hot porridge in front of him.

"Thank you, sir," John said as he gobbled down the porridge, wondering when he would eat next.

Before he left, John asked, "Where is the nearest Catholic church?"

The innkeeper replied, "Christ Church is nearby. Father Joseph Schneller is the pastor."

Following the innkeeper's directions, John quickly found the church only a few blocks from the inn. He entered and looked for the Blessed Sacrament. Spotting the red lamp by the tabernacle, he sighed with relief and knelt in one of the pews. John poured out his heart in prayer.

Jesus, thank you for bringing me here safely. Thank you for the kind people you have put in my path. Please take care of my family; I miss them so much. And continue to direct me, Lord. I only want to do your will.

Hearing footsteps, John turned and looked up—right into the eyes of a tall man wearing a black cassock.

"Hello. I haven't seen you here before," the priest said in English. "I'm Father Schneller."

"I'm John Neumann, a seminarian from Bohemia," John replied hesitantly, trying out his English for the first time in the United States. "I just arrived from Europe. It was a long trip! Can you hear my confession, Father?"

"I'd be happy to do that. Come with me," Father Schneller replied with a kind smile. Then he added in German, "And your English is excellent!"

After confession, John explained to Father Schneller why he had left Bohemia.

"Sounds like you need to speak with the bishop's Vicar General, Father Raffeiner," the priest told him. "He's at Saint Nicholas Church on East 2nd Street. He can help."

John went straight there and knocked on the rectory door. A priest opened it and asked, "Do you need something to eat, son?"

"No," John answered, "but I am looking for Father Raffeiner. Do you know him?"

"That's me," said the priest. Father Raffeiner led him into the cozy parlor. Offering John a chair, the priest asked, "How can I help you?"

John poured out his story. "I'm a seminarian from Bohemia. For the last few years I have felt that God was inviting me to work as a missionary. I want to be ordained a priest so I can serve God's people here in the United States. I know that many immigrants can't receive the sacraments due to the lack of priests." Here John paused, looked intently at the priest, and asked, "Did Bishop Dubois receive the letter that Canon Rass sent from Strasbourg? He sent it several months ago."

"Canon Rass? You know him?" Father Raffeiner responded with surprise. Seeing John's nod, the priest continued, "Bishop Dubois told me he received the application and sent a letter of acceptance to Canon Rass three weeks ago."

John took a deep breath and let the words sink in. He was accepted. Bishop Dubois had accepted him as a priest for the Diocese of New York! *Oh, the goodness and providence of God!* John thought happily.

"Didn't you receive the bishop's letter of acceptance?" Father Raffeiner asked.

"Letter of acceptance?" repeated John joyously. "I've been at sea for the past six weeks. I didn't even know of it!"

"Why didn't you wait for the bishop's answer before leaving your home?"

"I waited in Paris until my money ran so low that I had to decide whether to return to my family or trust in God and come to New York."

"You're quite an inspiration," said Father Raffeiner. "John, do you have credentials and letters of recommendation?"

Reaching into his satchel, John replied, "Yes, Father, they're right here."

Father Raffeiner read and reread the papers, not missing a word.

"Excellent, Mr. Neumann! Bishop Dubois will be very pleased. You're an answer to our prayers! We greatly need a priest for the missions near Buffalo. Many German people there will be so happy to have you among them."

John's heart leaped with joy. "I'm ready to go! I only need to be ordained."

"Well, let's go and tell Bishop Dubois our good news!" Father Raffeiner said as he rose from his chair. "We don't want to waste any time."

11

FRONTIER PASTOR

Just before Mass on the morning of June 25, 1836, John offered a prayer of deep gratitude. He had only been in the United States for a few weeks, and the day he had so long prepared for had finally arrived. Scanning the filled pews of St. Patrick's Church on Mulberry Street (New York's first cathedral, now called Old St. Patrick's), he thought, *Look at these good people. I'm so thankful they came. My only regret is that my family can't be here today to share in my joy. But I know they are here with me in their prayers.*

After the homily, John knelt in front of Bishop Dubois, who laid his hands on John's head. As the bishop said the prayer of consecration, John's heart overflowed with gratitude and joy. Next he received the chalice and ciborium from the bishop. John prayed, *Jesus, you have been so good and so faithful to me. Help me to be faithful to you! And help me to be a good and holy priest; that is all I want. . . .*

A couple of days after the ordination, John met with Bishop Dubois.

"Father Neumann, I'd like to send you to the New York region near Niagara Falls. The German immigrants there need a priest. Will you go and minister to them?"

"Yes, Bishop Dubois! That's why I came here!" John enthusiastically reached out and grasped the bishop's hand. "I've waited for this moment for a long time!"

"Good! You will make a wonderful priest and pastor," the bishop added. "Here's a ticket for a steamboat that will take you to your new home."

After Mass, on the morning of June 28, John grabbed his packed satchel, treasured books, and a Mass kit that contained all he would need to celebrate Mass. He had few personal belongings, but he liked it that way. *Less to distract me from God and less weight to carry!* he thought.

Arriving at State Street, John spotted the steamboat quickly filling with passengers. His steps picked up speed as he neared the dock. *I don't want to miss the boat!* he thought. As he boarded, John's heart pounded with excitement. *I'm a missionary priest, headed for my first mission! Thank you, Lord!*

John's first stop was the city of Rochester. Bishop Dubois had asked him to stay there for a week and minister to the many Germans there. And so John preached, baptized, and heard confessions—all day, every day!

At the week's end, John boarded a boat heading to Buffalo, a fast-growing town that was a halfway stop for thousands of immigrants headed West.

"Help at last!" Father Pax exclaimed as he spotted the young priest walking down the gangplank. "You must be Father Neumann," Father Pax said once John reached him. "I'm so glad to see you! I've been praying and asking the Lord for help."

John greeted him with a warm smile. As they walked to the parish, Father Pax told John about his failing health and exhaustion from all the work. He was the only priest working in a large area among the immigrants. The two men quickly made plans. Father Pax would be in charge of the parish in Buffalo; John would go to the more remote areas of what was called the Niagara frontier. John was strong and could handle the vast territory.

That evening after dinner he said to Father Pax, "I want to begin as soon as possible, so I'll leave tomorrow morning right after Mass. Souls are waiting!"

John's work brought him all over the wide plains of New York. Many times John walked, but sometimes he rode on horseback. With a Mass kit on his back, he would travel ten, twenty, or forty miles to reach the people. No distance was too far for John. He went willingly to each and every group of Catholics in the area. At first he lived in Williamsville, the central mission post. Then he moved to North Bush. The townspeople there had gifted their priest with five acres of land purchased with their hard-earned money. It took time, but with their help, John built a two-room log cabin. Now his home even had a thriving vegetable garden in the back!

Arriving home in the late afternoon one day after a long trip, John dismounted from his horse and said, "We're home, old girl." John tied his mare to a post, walked around to the back of his cabin, and returned with his arms full of fresh hay. "Here you go," he said. "Eat up! The worker is worth his wages!"

With that he turned to his little home and sighed with contentment. "It's so good to be home! I'm so blessed!"

*No distance was too far for John. He went willingly
to each and every group of Catholics in the area.*

John slowly opened the front door and stepped inside. The entrance was low and narrow, but since John was only a little over five feet tall, it made no difference to him. His eyes quickly scanned the cabin. They came to rest on the tabernacle in the corner of the room. There was the most important Person in the house—Jesus present in the Blessed Sacrament.

John approached and slowly sank to his knees saying aloud, "It is *so* good to come home to you, Jesus! I have so much to tell you."

12

SNOWSTORM

This snow is even worse than what we had in Bohemia, John thought. *It's so difficult to see. . . . I hope I don't get lost.* He was making his way through the woods toward Cayuga Creek. With his Mass kit strapped tightly to his back, he was making yet another trip to bring the sacraments to a group of Catholics. He could hardly see as the snow swirled all around him with great gusts of wind. As he rounded the bend in the road, he paused to straighten the pack on his back. In the distance he saw a log cabin with smoke curling up from the chimney. John sighed with relief. *Maybe the people in that cabin can help me find my way.*

John brushed the snow from his coat and knocked on the cabin's front door. When it slowly opened he said, "Excuse me, but I think I'm lost. May I step in out of the cold?" The woman did not respond, and her expression seemed unsure, so John continued, "I'm Father John Neumann, a Catholic priest."

"Father Neumann! Yes, we've heard about you. So good to see you!" the woman exclaimed as she threw open the cabin door. "Please come in out of the cold, Father. Welcome to our home." The woman bowed as John stepped through the doorway.

"May God bless this house and all who live in it," John said as he entered, his eyes quickly scanning the small cabin.

The poor dwelling had rough log walls, a dirt floor, and a gas lantern for light. A big, open fireplace provided the heat. Six young children were gathered around a wooden table in the middle of the cabin.

"Tommy," the woman called to the oldest, "get more wood for the fire. And please call your father. Tell him that our home is honored with the presence of a priest."

"Yes, Mother," Tommy said as he quickly rose from the table.

"Now, Father, let me take your pack." John slowly pulled the straps from his shoulders, as the woman helped. His hands were numb with cold.

"Goodness, your pack is heavy . . ." she remarked.

"Yes, it is, but it contains my Mass kit with my chalice, missal, and vestments," he said. "I was on my way to say Mass in Cayuga Creek, but I must have made a wrong turn."

"Cayuga Creek is far from here, Father. . . . Mass, you say? It's been months since we have been to Mass," she looked sadly at the ground. "Months."

Just then the door flew wide open, with a gust of cold wind following. In walked a big, sturdy man with soft, blue eyes. He set a pile of wood on the hearth, wiped the dirt on his trousers, and then extended his hand to John.

"I'm Michael O'Neill. Welcome to my home, Father. Have you been properly introduced to my family?" Turning to his wife and children, he began the introductions. "This is my wife, Mary."

His wife slowly curtsied. "Come, children, meet the good Father." The five children lined up in front of John. One by one they bowed or curtsied as their father called their names.

"I have a surprise for you all," said John as he reached deep into his pocket. "I always carry this with me, as I never am sure when I might need it." The delighted children crowded around Father John as he gave each one a piece of hard candy. John smiled widely, and his aches and tiredness seemed to disappear.

"Mary, have you offered Father anything to eat? He must be starving!" Michael continued, "Maybe something we could all enjoy!" The children eagerly agreed. John hadn't eaten all day, so a good meal was most welcome. Lunch was soon set on the table: big slices of bread, wedges of cheese, and piping hot tea.

"Father, can you lead us in a blessing?"

They all bowed their heads as John led them in prayer.

"Dear Lord, bless this wonderful family which has welcomed me into their home. Bless this delicious food we are about to receive, and bless Mary who has so lovingly prepared it." As John finished, he extended his hand in blessing over the food, while the children all said loudly, "Amen!"

After the meal, Michael and John sat by the fireplace sipping hot tea. "Now, Father, won't you spend the night with us?"

John said, "Thank you for the offer, Michael, but I cannot stay. I must be in Cayuga Creek by morning. I promised the people there I would bring them the sacraments and celebrate Mass. I'll have to leave tonight!"

Completely surprised, Michael turned to his wife.

Mary tried to convince John, "But Father, you can't make it in this weather. Cayuga Creek is ten miles northwest of us. You would surely be lost in the storm!"

"I must go, Mary. I need to be there by morning. And with God's help, I am sure I will make it. He has never let me down!"

Michael cleared his throat and nodded to his wife. Together they slipped into the back bedroom. While the parents consulted, the children gathered around John. "Don't go, Father. Please stay with us for the night."

They all pleaded. John smiled and told them, "I must go, my little friends. But I'll come back soon and celebrate Mass with your family. How about that?"

Just then Michael and Mary reappeared. "Father Neumann!" Michael said with determination in his voice. "To get to Cayuga Creek tonight is impossible. But I have an idea. Our neighbor down the road has a horse and sleigh, and I know that he'll be happy to lend it to us. Stay with us tonight, and early tomorrow morning we can all ride to Mass together in his sleigh."

John thought for a moment and then nodded. "Yes, I will stay. Thank you so much, Michael and Mary." The children all clapped with delight.

"Let's all say a Rosary," suggested John later that evening, just before the family went to bed. "We have much to be grateful for. We can thank our Blessed Mother for her motherly care and protection." They all knelt on the dirt floor as the fire crackled in the fireplace and the wind whistled outside.

"Hail Mary, full of grace . . ." they all prayed.

After they finished praying, Mary set up a makeshift bed near the fireplace for John, as the children climbed to the loft above.

"Thank you, Father John, for this evening. It was wonderful to pray together."

John smiled, "Thank the good Lord. It's all his doing! Now I must get some sleep."

Michael and Mary politely nodded and retired to their room. "See you in the morning, Father. Sleep well."

"I will, my friends. I will."

Before John went to sleep he thanked God for sending him to this kind and generous family. He also said a prayer that God had heard many times before: *"Please send me some help. This good family has not seen a priest in months. It is difficult for me to do all of this work on my own!"* John thought of all the letters he had already sent to Bohemia and Germany asking for help—but no help ever arrived.

Sometimes John wondered if he should have joined a community of priests who would do this kind of work together. He had met priests from a community called the Redemptorists who lived together and did missionary work. *I would enjoy doing this work with others, as part of a community,* he thought. *But no matter, I need to focus on what is needed now. Please, Lord, send me some help!*

John went to sleep. Little did he know that someone he knew very well would soon arrive to help him.

13

THE BIG SURPRISE!

"Wenzel, I can hardly believe you're here!" John hugged his younger brother tightly. It was September 1839. John had often written to his brother asking him to come to the United States to help. After several letters back and forth, Wenzel had decided to save money and make the long trip to help John with his missionary work. John could hardly believe it; help had arrived at last!

"Please, tell me about the family. How are they doing?" John asked.

"Believe me, everyone misses you very much," responded Wenzel. "They pray for you every day."

"I miss them too, and pray for them always," John said with sadness. "But I'm so glad you're here! We have lots to catch up on. First, I want you to meet Father Pax. Then, we'll travel on to North Bush where I live. How does that sound?"

"Fantastic," said Wenzel with a big smile on his face. He was happy to see John. It had been so long.

Wenzel and John returned home and immediately set to work. Under Wenzel's constant care, the small log cabin became even more like a home. The vegetable garden flourished, and Wenzel often cooked dinner after he returned from teaching at two nearby schools. John was so happy to have his brother there, not just to help out with work but to have someone to confide in when things were difficult.

"Wenzel, it's such a big help that you're teaching catechism to the children," John said one evening as they ate supper. "I loved teaching the children myself," he continued, "but when you teach, it allows me more time to travel to bring the sacraments to all the people who need them."

"I enjoy teaching the children, John," smiled Wenzel contentedly. "I've even been thinking that one day I might become a priest like you! I love this life."

"That would be great, Wenzel, but being a priest is not always easy," John replied. "In fact, today that old sheepherder who drinks too much threatened to kill me and then followed me for almost a mile with his rifle pointed at me! But I just laughed it off."

"What? John, that's not funny at all!" said Wenzel with concern in his voice.

"Oh, you are right. It wasn't funny at the time, but I couldn't help but laugh once I was free of him," said John lightheartedly.

One day, John returned from a long trip looking very weak and exhausted. His face was flushed with fever and his eyes were glazed. As soon as he entered the cabin, he went straight to bed.

"Wenzel, my head is pounding and I'm hot all over."

"Don't worry, big brother," Wenzel assured him. "I'll take care of you. I'll make some chicken soup—remember how Mama always made soup when we didn't feel well?"

John stayed in bed for the rest of that day, and the next. The great distances that he traveled to reach his people, along with small amounts of food and rest, had taken their toll. John's illness stretched on for several weeks and then into months! Wenzel ended up caring for John for three long months.

One day, feeling stronger at last, John rose from bed and took a seat. "Wenzel, can you come here? I need to speak with you."

Wenzel quickly grabbed one of the wooden chairs and came closer. "What is it, John?" he asked, taking a seat. Silence filled the room as Wenzel waited patiently for his brother to speak. Finally Wenzel prodded, "Well John, what did you want to tell me?"

Speaking slowly and clearly, John began. "As I lay sick in bed these past three months, I've had plenty of time to think and pray . . . about my future." Wenzel shifted in the chair uneasily. "Wenzel, there's no easy way to say this. . . . I've decided to leave this area and join a community of priests, the Redemptorists."

Wenzel's eyes opened wide in disbelief. "The Redemptorists? But why, John? What will that mean?"

"It means that I will live in a community with other priests and brothers and I will take vows of poverty, chastity, and obedience. I will no longer have my own money and I will work under the direction of a superior. I'll still be a priest doing missionary work, but I think God is calling me to this life. And I want to follow his will. I want to become holy, Wenzel. I want to become a saint!"

Wenzel just sat and listened to his brother with a puzzled, look on his face.

"I have been looking into the different religious communities that serve in the United States. And I feel drawn to the spirit of Saint Alphonsus, the founder of the Redemptorists. I want to serve the poor and those people who most need spiritual help. And I want to work with other priests, to live in a community." John paused and looked at Wenzel, who seemed stunned.

John continued, "I have been thinking about this for some time. I'm planning to write to Father Proust, the head of the Redemptorist Order, in Baltimore to ask him for admission."

"But John, that means that you will leave me here in North Bush," Wenzel said.

"I was hoping that you would think about coming with me."

Wenzel gasped. John continued, "I understand if you cannot. But I need to do this."

Wenzel said nothing. John watched as Wenzel got up and left the cabin. John felt terrible. He did not mean to hurt Wenzel; that was the last thing he wanted. John took out his rosary and began to pray.

14

A NEW BEGINNING

I wonder what Wenzel has been up to? John thought as he dismounted from his horse after a long trip. He could hear singing and noticed smoke rising from his cabin's chimney. He opened the door and looked inside in amazement. The table was all set for dinner, and the aroma of delicious food wafted through the air.

"John, we're having a feast tonight!" Wenzel said cheerfully. "A feast of *veprove se zelim* (pork with cabbage and potatoes), just like Mama used to make back home!"

John just stood in the doorway confused. "When I left, you seemed so quiet and unhappy at my news," John told his brother "It's good to see you happy again! What are we celebrating?"

Wenzel looked up from the stove, smiled, and said, "While you were gone this week, I went to Buffalo."

"Yes?" said John.

"And while I was there, I had a long talk with Father Pax." Wenzel's voice became serious. "I want to grow closer to God, too. I had thought about becoming a priest but it never seemed right. Father Pax and I talked about the vocation of a religious brother, a *Redemptorist* religious brother. I believe that this may be what God is calling me to do. I've decided to enter the Redemptorists as a postulant and see if God is calling me there."

John's mouth dropped wide open. "A Redemptorist like me! That's wonderful news, Wenzel!"

John hugged his younger brother and said, "I'm so happy! If it is God's will, we'll be brothers by blood and brothers in the Redemptorist Order!"

"We've been waiting for you, Father Neumann," said Father Czackert (zak-ert) as he extended his hand. "Welcome to the Redemptorist family. You are our first novice in the United States!"

It was October 18, 1840, and John had just arrived at the Church of St. Philomena in Pittsburgh.

"Thank you, Father Czackert. I am so glad to be here," said John.

"Where is your brother Wenceslaus? I heard he was going to join us too," Father Czackert said.

"Wenzel is still in North Bush. He needed to pack and wrap up some things. But he will be here soon," John reassured him.

Several days after arriving in Pittsburgh, John received the long black robe of the Redemptorists in a simple ceremony. Bowing his head, John silently prayed, *Now I'm officially a part of this religious community! Thank you, Lord, thank you for bringing me here to serve the poor and do your will.*

John was already a priest so he was asked to immediately set to work helping in the parishes. Since John was a novice, he had hoped for more preparation and instruction. But this was not to be, at least for now. John worked hard in the Redemptorist parishes and was also asked to move quite often from one community to another. Wenzel had arrived from North Bush and had joined just as he had promised, but John was rarely assigned to the same place as his brother. John had hoped to be with Wenzel more often and he felt disappointed. But he prayed, *Jesus, I thought I would have more time for prayer and learning about the mission and spiri-*

tuality of the Redemptorists. And I miss Wenzel. I was used to his company! But I guess it is not to be. I trust you, Jesus; your will be done.

One evening after supper, all of the priests were laughing and telling stories, but John was especially quiet.

"What's the matter, Father Neumann? Is something bothering you?" asked Father Czackert.

"It's nothing, really," responded John. "I just had a strange dream last night."

"Dream?" said Father Czackert, raising his eyebrows. "Tell us about it."

John looked down for a moment feeling embarrassed. Then, he said, "In my dream I was sitting at my desk. All of a sudden a bishop came into my room. He seemed to know me. He sat down beside my desk. . . . Then he said . . ." John couldn't go on.

"Speak up, Father Neumann. Don't leave us in suspense!"

The words rushed out of John's mouth. "In my dream the bishop said a diocese needed a bishop and he wanted to send my name to the pope!"

No one said a word. All the priests knew that when a Redemptorist priest takes a vow of poverty it rules out assignments like becoming a bishop, unless the pope himself orders the priest to accept. Father Czackert raised his eyebrows and looked around the table at the other priests. Then he turned to John and asked warily, "And then?"

"I froze," said John. "I begged him not to send my name to Rome. But he persisted. Then he took off the cross he was wearing and tried to place it over my shoulders. That's when I woke up."

Father Czackert was not impressed. "I can't believe you would speak openly of becoming a bishop, and as a novice who just joined our order! No Redemptorist should even dream of becoming a bishop." The other Redemptorists at the table nodded in agreement. Father Czackert continued, "I hope that your proud fantasies disappear soon. Pray that you persevere as a good, simple Redemptorist priest!"

John's face flushed red and he felt his heart beating quickly, but he nodded and simply said, "I will pray that God grants me that grace." John was upset, but he knew that he didn't want to be a bishop and that his

Redemptorist brothers had misunderstood him.

As the months passed, John began to doubt his decision. *Should I have left my work as a priest in New York? I love serving the people with the Redemptorists and teaching the children catechism, but it seems like all I do is work! I have hardly any time for prayer.* As he thought this over one night after a long day, he knelt before the Blessed Sacrament and prayed.

Jesus, I feel very alone with little guidance and direction. Is it really your will for me to remain with the Redemptorists?

Finally John told Father Tschenhens (TSCHEN-henz), the Redemptorist who heard John's confessions, about how he was feeling. As John shared his many difficulties, Father Tschenhens realized that he had to address this situation.

"Father Neumann, I will arrange for you to go to Saint Alphonsus Church in Baltimore. You'll have more time to pray and study, and you can finish your novitiate in peace there."

When John heard Father Tschenhens' welcome words, a deep sense of relief and peace filled his heart. *God is looking after me,* he realized. *I must trust that he'll provide for me as he always has. Thank you, Jesus, for this gift of time to see what you really want from me.*

Help me to know whether or not you want me to make my vows as a Redemptorist.

John arrived in Baltimore in December. He prayed a lot during this time. Sometimes he prayed late into the night. After making a fourteen-day retreat, John's doubts lifted.

"Thank you, Jesus, for helping me," John prayed. "Now I can see clearly that you are calling me to be a Redemptorist. I want to do your will."

At St. James Church in Baltimore, John made his profession of vows on January 16, 1842. Now he was a Redemptorist, the first to make his vows in the United States! John was excited to begin this new phase in his life. But little did he know that God had even more changes in store for him.

15

AN UNEXPECTED REQUEST

John loved being a Redemptorist priest. The people knew him as a holy confessor and good preacher. But he most enjoyed his work among the poorest of the poor, including prisoners and hardened criminals.

One day his superior asked, "Father Neumann, can you go to the gallows tomorrow? A criminal is going to be hanged."

"Of course," said John.

The next day, John headed to the gallows early in the morning and approached the supervising officer and asked to see the man.

"Sure, Father," the officer said. "But he will never talk to you. He killed his first wife and then his second. The man is evil, absolutely unredeemable."

"No one is beyond the power of Jesus," John said quietly.

John approached the man who was standing with his hands tied behind his back. His clothes were dirty and ripped, and he was looking at the ground.

"Hello, friend. I've come to hear your confession," said John.

The man glared at John and spit on the ground, "Friend? No one is my friend."

"Jesus is your friend and he died for your sins. If you repent now, he will forgive you," said John.

"I cannot be forgiven, priest. I'm an evil man," said the criminal, his voice mournfully cracking for an instant.

"You are wrong. No sin is too great for God to forgive," John insisted.

The criminal looked up at John with hope in his eye. "Okay, priest, I want to tell God how sorry I am for my sins before I die."

John smiled and leaned closer to the man so that he could listen to his confession.

Toward the end of 1851, the new Archbishop of Baltimore, Francis Patrick Kenrick, would walk each week from the cathedral to the rectory at St. Alphonsus so that John could hear his confession.

"You're very wise, Father Neumann. You make everything sound so simple!" said the archbishop one day after confession; then half jokingly he added, "You should be a bishop yourself!"

"No, thank you," said John. "I'll leave that job to you!"

The archbishop smiled and grew thoughtful. Then he said, "You know, I just left Philadelphia to become the bishop here. That diocese now needs a bishop to replace me. I've been wondering if I should recommend you!"

"Oh no, please don't do that! I love being a simple priest," John protested nervously.

"What is important is whether or not *God* wills it," said the archbishop. "I'll pray about this."

As the archbishop rose to leave, John remembered the dream he had had as a novice in Pittsburgh. During the next few weeks John hoped and prayed that Archbishop Kenrick would forget the idea to recommend him as bishop. But soon he was dismayed to hear that his name was on a list of potential bishops that was sent to Rome.

Some people knew that John was a good and holy man, and they hoped the pope would make him a bishop. Others thought the idea was outrageous. "Bishops in the eastern United States have always been

French, Irish, or American—never from Bohemia!" said one merchant.

Someone else added, "He's so unrefined. He feels more comfortable on a farm than in this city. He'll never fit in with the Philadelphia rich and elite."

"Some anti-Catholic groups are active in Philadelphia. They even burned down several Catholic churches not so long ago. Could Father Neumann handle that?" another person objected.

John frantically wrote to his superior in Rome to ask him to stop the appointment. But the decision was up to Pope Pius IX. The pope had heard about John's holiness, his language skills, and his experience with many different cultures. Impressed with all of this, he chose to name John the fourth bishop of Philadelphia.

When Archbishop Kenrick received the pope's decision, he decided to walk to St. Alphonsus to deliver the news in person. After knocking on the rectory door, the archbishop was ushered in and went to John's room as he normally did for confession. But John was not there. So Archbishop Kenrick thought, *I'll leave my cross and bishop's ring on his reading table. Surely John will recognize them and get the message!*

When John returned home that evening, the sparkle of the ring in his room caught his eye. John called the brother who tended the door and asked him anxiously, "Who has been here?"

"Archbishop Kenrick," responded the porter. After the brother left, John fell to his knees.

On Sunday, March 28, 1852, which was also John's birthday, people from all over the city streamed toward St. Alphonsus to see John made a bishop. One person who badly wanted to be there could not make it. Wenzel was now stationed with the Redemptorists in Detroit, and the cost and long distance made it impossible for him to travel to Baltimore.

During his episcopal ordination at the hands of his friend, Archbishop Kenrick, John prayed for the strength to accept the cross God had given him. For his episcopal motto he chose: "Passion of Christ, strengthen me," for it said best what he felt inside.

At the reception afterward, John spotted a group of parishioners. The smiling group carried a beautifully wrapped package. As the parishioners came closer, one of them handed him the package and said, "Father Neumann—I mean, *Bishop* Neumann, we have a gift for you."

John smiled broadly. He loved these good people. Carefully removing the paper, he discovered a beautiful gold chalice. "This is exquisite! I'll always remember my good friends from here at St. Alphonsus. Thank you so much! May God bless you." Then, raising his hand over the group, he gave them a blessing.

Despite the love and support of so many wonderful people, John was still very much afraid of his future. He would also miss his Redemptorist community. Late that evening, John went back to the now empty church.

Kneeling in front of the tabernacle he prayed, *Jesus, please help me! I am overwhelmed whenever I think of all the responsibilities I'll have. I will be in charge of the churches in most of Pennsylvania, Delaware, and parts of New Jersey. So many Catholics who need good leadership! I've always relied on your Divine Providence; help me to keep on doing that. I trust that this is your plan and that with your grace I will be a good bishop.*

John left for Philadelphia the next day, trusting in God despite his fears.

16

PHILADELPHIA

As John rode on the train to Philadelphia, worries crowded his mind. He decided to pray, so he took out his rosary beads. As he said the words of the Hail Mary, a deep peace came over him.

God has taken care of me so far and given me the grace to do everything he has asked of me. Why should I doubt him now?

A few hours later, John stepped off the train in Philadelphia to the sound of loud clapping and cheers. A large group of priests had come to meet him! John felt his anxiety lessen when he saw the happy faces of the priests of his new diocese.

"Thank you for coming!" said John, beaming with joy.

Father Sourin stepped forward to greet him. He was a burly man with a twinkle in his eye. "Bishop Neumann, I am Father Sourin. I was in charge of the diocese while we were waiting for a bishop."

"I wish I could have left you in charge!" joked John.

Father Sourin laughed. He knew John had accepted his role as bishop reluctantly. "No, it is much better that you have come. We have been eagerly awaiting a new bishop! Some of the other priests wanted to have a parade to welcome you, but I heard that you wouldn't like that."

"I'm so glad that you did something simple," responded the new bishop. "I am just an immigrant priest happy to serve God's people."

"Yes, we knew you would feel that way," Father Sourin continued. "So, in your honor, the money we would have spent on a parade is going toward building a new school."

"That is truly the best gift I could receive. Thank you!" John replied.

That night, after John attended a reception in his honor, he returned to his new residence on Logan Square. "I'm so exhausted." John chuckled to himself. "These social events really tire me out. But I'd better get used to them!"

John went to bed, but not to sleep. Thoughts of his new large diocese filled his mind. So many immigrants from Europe were streaming into the Philadelphia area. John knew he would have many challenges to face in the days and months ahead. He also knew who would help him: Jesus.

Lord, I trust you. I know we'll face all these challenges together. But now I need to get some sleep, so good night, Jesus.

John rolled over and drifted off.

The next day, John was full of energy and excitement.

"Father Sourin, can you come with me to visit the parishes, schools, and hospitals of the diocese? You know Philadelphia well and I'm really eager to get to know everything and everyone!"

"I'd be delighted to join you," replied Father Sourin. "When shall we begin, Bishop Neumann?"

"There's no moment like the present," John said with a big smile.

"Let's start with a visit to St. Joseph's School," said Father Sourin. "We'll surprise the children and teachers."

"That's a wonderful idea," John responded. "I used to teach catechism sometimes when I was in New York, so this will be a real treat for me."

A few days after visiting the school, John told Father Sourin, "I'd love to visit the sick at St. Joseph's Hospital."

"Of course, we can go this afternoon," said Father Sourin warmly. He was getting used to John's constant desire to meet the people and to get to know his diocese.

That afternoon, John walked through the hospital wards giving encouragement. "Jesus loves you so very much. He suffers with you and is always by your side."

Spotting one man with gray hair and a wrinkled, sad face, John touched his crucifix to the man's lips and said, "Here, kiss my crucifix. Unite all your suffering with that of Jesus. Take courage. Jesus has a beautiful reward waiting for you in heaven." John encouraged everyone he saw that day. It made no difference what age, race, or religion they were—to him they were all God's children.

John could see so many needs as he toured his city and diocese. Several of the various language groups in his diocese did not have churches or schools. He knew that he would need a lot of help in the days to come.

John also immediately noticed that a large number of the Irish people in his diocese did not speak English. Although he could speak the languages of almost all the other immigrants he met, he didn't know

Irish Gaelic. He immediately began to study it so that he could hear the confessions of his Irish people.

I have learned plenty of other languages with the help of God's grace, what's one more? God, you have given me this job, now please give me the grace to learn this language quickly! John laughed to himself.

He learned the language so well that one day after hearing a woman's confession in Irish, she left the confessional and then exclaimed loudly to the people waiting, "Thanks be to God! We have an Irish bishop!"

Inside the confessional, John couldn't help but laugh heartily. "Oh God, you always provide!"

17

SECRETS OF SUCCESS

John spent five months of his first three years as bishop on the road. He traveled by train, on foot, and in bumpy stagecoaches to visit his large diocese. He loved visiting and experiencing the simple life of his people. Rain, snow, mountains, subzero temperatures, and even summer's heat didn't stop him. On one visit to a rural parish, the local pastor picked him up in a wagon full of smelly manure! John laughed and jumped on the wagon without any complaint; he didn't want fanfare because he was a bishop.

At a small, rural German parish near Lancaster, Pennsylvania John told the pastor, "I love visiting with the people. This is my favorite part of being bishop! Can I show you the schedule I've prepared?"

"Of course, Bishop Neumann. The people have been eagerly awaiting your visit for weeks!"

Reaching into his worn satchel, John retrieved a few handwritten papers. "First I'd like to celebrate Mass each morning—

preaching in German. And I would like to give a talk about the Eucharist. It's so important that the people get to know Jesus in the Blessed Sacrament—more important than anything else."

"Yes, of course, Bishop Neumann," the pastor replied.

"I'll visit the sick of the parish during the day, as well as the poor. And then I'd like to teach the children catechism at least one day. I am writing a catechism in German, and I want to test out the material! Then, in the evening we can meet for night prayer—"

"Bishop Neumann," the pastor interrupted, "you have planned so much, but I hope you'll also be able to relax and enjoy yourself. Some ladies from the parish have been planning to serve you delicious meals!"

John said, "What a treat! I miss German food! I think I'm going to enjoy my visit with you very much!"

One day, just after returning to Philadelphia from one of his trips, John went to breakfast with a pensive look on his face. He had been praying in the chapel as he almost always did at the beginning of the day.

"Father Sourin, I have been thinking about what our priorities should be, and after praying about it, I think we must get to work and build more schools for the children," said John. "We must do all we can to educate our children in the faith."

"I agree, Bishop Neumann," said Father Sourin. "Some teachers in the public schools here have anti-Catholic views and pass those on to their students. We need our own Catholic schools. The children should go to school where their faith will be strengthened, not attacked."

"And we need more churches for the immigrant communities. Language helps to preserve the faith," John added. "We must give our immigrant people their own churches and priests who can speak their language."

John quickly set to work to build more churches and parish schools. As he traveled around the diocese, he encouraged the priests and people of the diocese to work together. In just a little over two years the number of children enrolled in Catholic schools in his diocese went from 500 to 9,000. John would eventually supervise the building of almost one hundred schools. During the same time period, he oversaw the completion of six churches, the rebuilding of six others, and the addition of thirty new churches to the diocese. Fifty churches were eventually built during his time as bishop.

Everyone who observed John was amazed at his energy. People found it difficult to say no when the persistent, holy bishop would ask them to support building a school or a parish. Yet, when he was praised, John immediately gave the credit to others. "Yes, I have worked hard," he would say, "but the pastors and the generous people have sacrificed even more. With God's help, together we have built these schools and churches for our children."

But John did do plenty, and everyone knew it. He wrote letters to his pastors and often encouraged the people to be generous by volunteering for their parishes and giving their money and talent to new projects.

"God deserves only the best. Together we can build him a beautiful house! He will repay us in heaven!" he exclaimed one Sunday from the church pulpit in Danville. Knowing that many of the people were unsure how they could support him and still care for their families, he added, "This is God's work, and we can trust that he will help us succeed!"

When John finished his homily, he noticed a woman in the front row clutching a handkerchief and crying. *I hope she is crying for joy!* thought John. Then he looked around and, to his embarrassment, he noticed that almost everyone in the church had tears rolling down their cheeks. When the collection baskets went around the church, everyone contributed eagerly.

Thank you, Lord, for moving their hearts to be so generous! he prayed.

John knew that whatever he accomplished was due only to God's grace. Ever grateful, he thanked and praised God for all of those amazing things. But John especially had at heart one special project. He couldn't stop thinking about it. Building schools and churches was important. But buildings didn't matter if the people didn't know Jesus. John wanted to do something to encourage the people to know Jesus better.

The only problem was that his plan might be dangerous.

18

FORTY HOURS WITH JESUS

Early one morning, as usual, John went to pray before the Blessed Sacrament.

"Jesus, thank you for all that you have done to help me in my work as bishop," John prayed aloud. "We have done so much, building schools and teaching the people. But I want above all to help the people know and love you in the Eucharist. Please guide me and help me to know how to best do this."

As John prayed, the idea he had been thinking about became clearer. The next day Father Sourin came to ask him something about the finances needed for building a school at a nearby parish. After they had discussed the necessary details, John decided he would ask Father Sourin what he thought of his idea.

"Father Sourin, I want to do something that will help the people in their prayer life. The Eucharist is the center of our faith. I've been thinking about an idea to help teach people the importance of the Eucharist and strengthen their faith in the real presence of Jesus."

Father Sourin nodded. Wondering what idea had the bishop so excited, he asked, "What do you have in mind?"

"I have heard about this practice, the Forty Hours' Devotion to the Eucharist, and I would like to introduce it to our people," said John excitedly.

"I think I've heard of that devotion, but what is it exactly?" responded Father Sourin curiously.

"We would encourage every parish at a certain time in the year to have forty continuous hours of adoration of Jesus in the Blessed Sacrament," John explained. "We would have processions in the street with the Eucharist, and then people could sign up to come and pray for one of the forty hours that the Eucharist would be available in every church! The Eucharist would be outside of the tabernacle, in a monstrance, available for everyone to see."

"What a wonderful idea! It's very important to teach the people about prayer and the Eucharist." Then Father Sourin paused a moment before adding, "But I worry about vandalism and violence. Some people in Philadelphia greatly oppose the Catholic faith. As you know, before you arrived some of our churches were burned down."

John looked disappointed, but then he agreed, "Yes, you are right. We must think about this before making any decisions. Thank you for your input, Father Sourin."

For days John thought about his idea. He prayed before the Blessed Sacrament, asking Jesus to help him know what to do.

Would beginning the Forty Hours' Devotion expose the Blessed Sacrament to danger? I want my people to adore you, Jesus, not expose you or any of my people to danger!

John also asked some of the priests in the diocese what they thought. Some were excited.

One priest said, "This devotion will surely help the people to experience the goodness of God. All our school buildings and churches mean nothing if our people aren't close friends of Jesus!"

But others had the same concerns as Father Sourin. One priest responded to John's idea with deep apprehension. "I would like to do something like this, but just a few years ago some people started riots against the Church. What will they do when we have a procession in the streets with the Blessed Sacrament? I just wonder if it's the right time. . . ."

John didn't know what to do. But one night a strange thing happened. As he was working on some papers by candlelight, he fell asleep at his desk. The candle burned so low that it charred some of the papers. But when he awoke, he could still read the words on the paper, even though the candle was still burning. It was amazing that the papers had not gone up in flames! He immediately fell on his knees.

Dear Jesus, thank you for keeping me safe. You are so very good to me!

At that moment John seemed to hear God say to him, "See how the fire burns without destroying the writing on the paper? In the same way, I will protect my people from harm and pour out my grace in the Blessed Sacrament. Don't be afraid to carry out your plans."

John felt peaceful after hearing these words in prayer, and the next morning he told Father Sourin that he had decided to move ahead. John began the Forty Hours' Devotion in 1853 on the Feast of Corpus Christi. It was a happy day for the diocese.

John was so grateful to God. He spent most of the three days' devotion in the Church of St. Philip Neri. Praying before the Blessed Sacrament, he thanked Jesus from the bottom of his heart. *Thank you, Jesus, for giving me the courage to do this for you. Thank you for all the grace you are pouring out on your people. Thank you for your continued providence and care.* The event was a success and no one made trouble. John thought, *As he always does, Jesus kept his word.* John felt very happy. Things were going well in the diocese and he rejoiced to help his people grow in their devotion to the holy Eucharist.

God is so good, he thought. *So many blessings! And I received an invitation recently to something very special, so I will have another really big blessing soon. I can't wait!*

19

A VISIT TO ROME

One day John called Father Sourin and told him, "I've been invited to Rome to hear Pope Pius IX proclaim the dogma that Mary was free from all sin from the moment of conception in her mother's womb! And full of grace, full of divine life!" John exclaimed excitedly. "What an amazing opportunity this is!"

"It's such a special event for the Church," Father Sourin replied. "The dogma of the Immaculate Conception shows how important Mary's role was. God prepared her to be the mother of his Son. As a bishop it's important that you go. Still, I know it will be hard for you to be away from the people," Father Sourin said.

"But they're in good hands. With you taking care of the diocese while I'm away, I don't have to worry." John smiled.

"I'll be praying that you have a wonderful visit with your family as well. I am glad you will be able to see them," Father Sourin added. He handed John a bag with some supplies, saying, "This is for you—a little snack for your trip!"

"Thank you. Edward, I want to tell you . . ." John paused as Father Sourin smiled in slight surprise at being called by his first name, ". . . that you have been such an invaluable help to me over these past few years. You know that, don't you?" John said, patting his friend on the shoulder.

"Oh, don't get sentimental on me!" laughed Father Sourin. "I have been happy to help you, Bishop Neumann. I know you didn't want this job, but God certainly wanted you to have it. You are a wonderful bishop and I am honored to work with you." After that John headed to the docks.

As he boarded the *U.S.S. Union* later that morning, the sun shone brightly. The big ship was bound for the busy port of Le Havre, France. It would be a much faster trip than the one John made to the United States. This voyage would take only seventeen days compared to the forty days he had spent on board the *Europa*.

John had lots of time to think and reflect as he sailed to Europe. He thought of the many changes in his life during the past eighteen years. He thought of his family and how much he had missed them.

I only wish that my dear mother were still alive to see me celebrate Mass. It will be bittersweet to see my family without my loving mother.

One day, John was standing out on deck looking at the sun just beginning to rise. Then, bowing his head in thanksgiving and gratitude, John prayed.

Lord, you've been so good to me. When I traveled to the United States on the Europa *I didn't even know if I'd ever be ordained. But you took care of me and even led me to become a bishop, despite how unworthy I am. And now you're giving me the opportunity to go to Rome and visit my family and friends. Thank you for blessing me!*

John stayed in Rome for two months, living with the Redemptorist community of Santa Maria in Monterone. As he often did, John would wear a simple black, threadbare cassock, rather than a bishop's cassock with colored buttons and a sash.

"John, why aren't you dressed like a bishop?" asked one of his Redemptorist brothers.

"I prefer it this way. At heart, all I've ever wanted is to be a simple priest," John replied with a smile.

On the big day, December 8, 1854, thousands of people crowded into St. Peter's Basilica. Pope Pius IX moved slowly down the long center aisle of St. Peter's as over 50,000 people gathered for the Mass. John joined in singing the Litany of the Saints. After the Gospel was proclaimed in Latin and Greek, Cardinal Macchi and several archbishops and bishops walked over to the pope's chair. He asked the Holy Father to define the doctrine of Mary's Immaculate Conception as infallible. Pope Pius IX replied, "First, it is necessary to invoke the Holy Spirit.

"Come, Holy Spirit," Pope Pius IX prayed. Soon everyone in St. Peter's joined him in prayer: *Come, Holy Spirit!*

The pope rose slowly from his chair and made the declaration, "We declare that through the power of Jesus' death and resurrection, the Blessed Virgin Mary was preserved from sin and filled with grace from the first moment of her conception in order to prepare her to say 'yes' to her role as the Mother of God."

His words echoed throughout the vast cathedral. Guns boomed loudly from nearby San Angelo's Castle. The pope and the

Church wanted the whole world to hear the news.

Later that night, John knelt in the Redemptorist chapel and prayed before the tabernacle. *Thank you, Lord, for allowing me to be present on this holy day. And thank you, Mary, for saying "yes" to the Lord and for giving birth to God's Son. It was your Immaculate Conception that prepared you to say "yes" and to be the Mother of God.* John spent a while longer in the chapel, sitting in silence and drinking in the peace.

But by the next day, the peace he had felt the evening before had dissipated. He was feeling nervous. John was excited to visit his family. He hadn't seen them in such a long time! But first, he needed to make one *very* important visit.

20

VISITS WITH FRIENDS

John's heart pounded as he walked down the long hallway. This was the day when he would meet with Pope Pius IX for his *ad limina* visit and tell the Holy Father about his large diocese.

Will the pope be pleased with what we've done in the diocese of Philadelphia? John wondered as he entered the large ornate room.

Pius IX smiled warmly as John entered. "Bishop Neumann of Philadelphia, isn't obedience always best?" The pope said with a teasing look in his eyes.

"Yes, Your Holiness!" John laughed, knowing exactly what he meant. The pope was referring to John's reluctance to accept the office as bishop of Philadelphia several years before.

"Come, sit here," the pope said as he motioned to a chair nearby. John took a seat as the pope continued. "Bishop Neumann, I like what I read in your report; you have done much good in Philadelphia. I am most pleased with the many new churches and schools you've built for the immigrants. In just a little over two years the number of children enrolled in Catholic schools in your diocese have gone from 500 to 9,000. That's amazing!"

"Your Holiness, we've done a lot, but there's still much more to do! Sometimes I feel overwhelmed with the task before me. At the moment I have been preoccupied with the need to provide care for German children who have been orphaned."

"Yes, that is understandable . . ." the pope said as he looked intently at John. "I am wondering, do you have any religious sisters in your diocese who could help with this task?"

John quickly responded. "Not really, Your Holiness. . . ."

"Then maybe you can start an order in your diocese that can serve German orphans. Surely God is calling women religious to serve him in this way," the pope replied.

John looked at the pope with surprise and said, "Your Holiness, this is truly amazing. A priest in my diocese is actually working now with some women who want to help the poor. They would like to become Franciscans."

"Well this must be God's will then!" the pope responded. "See to it that this work is begun."

John hadn't come to Rome to ask the Holy Father if he could begin a new community of religious sisters, but it seemed clear that this is what God wanted.

"Yes, Your Holiness," John agreed. John and the pope continued to talk about the diocese, and when the meeting ended, John asked, "Can you please give me your blessing before I leave? I'm going to need it!"

"Yes, of course, my son."

After John left Rome, he traveled to a town near Vienna to see someone he had not seen in many years.

The coach stopped near the front entrance of the Graz Seminary and John climbed out. Just as he was exiting the coach, John heard a familiar voice.

"Still dressing in your worn black cassock, John? I should've known you wouldn't wear the bishop's cassock!" Adalbert gave John a welcoming hug.

"Adalbert, it has been so long!" exclaimed John.

"You haven't changed a bit," Adalbert said as he reached for John's bag.

John smiled at his old friend's teasing. "You're right. Some things don't change . . . but some do, *Father* Adalbert! When I left we were both seminarians, and now look at you! Spiritual director for the seminarians here! We have a lot to catch up on, don't we?!"

After giving John a tour of the seminary, and introducing him to a number of priests, Adalbert invited John into the parlor. "I know you must be tired from all the traveling, but I want to hear all about your time in Rome and the United States."

The two friends talked long into the night. Finally Adalbert rose from his chair, lantern in hand, and said, "We had best call it a night, don't you think, old friend? We can go for a walk in the morning after Mass, before the sleigh comes and you need to leave."

After saying farewell to Aldabert, John got on the sleigh and headed to Budweis. It had been such a consolation to see Adalbert after these many years. He was doing well.

Life at the Graz Seminary was a good fit, and John was grateful his friend was happy.

After that, John went to the Budweis Seminary. He met a few old friends and reminisced about his days there. He didn't stay long, though, because he was only a short trip away from home. His heart longed to see his family again. What would they be like after so many years?

21

HOME AGAIN

As John left Budweis in a sleigh that evening, he breathed in the cool, crisp air. When he neared Nettolitz (NEH-toe-leets), a town not far from Prachatitz, he noticed people kneeling in the snow along the road-side.

What are they doing? he wondered. Then he realized with embarrassment that they were there to see him.

One person begged from the side of the road, "Please, Bishop Neumann, give us your blessing."

John raised his hand and made the Sign of the Cross over the kneeling faithful.

As the sleigh drew into Nettolitz, the church bells rang loudly. People streamed from their homes and waved at John.

The sleigh stopped in front of a crowd of people waving. A parish priest stepped forward from the crowd and spoke. "Bishop Neumann, we would be honored if you stayed here tonight. Then you'll be well rested to greet your family tomorrow in Prachatitz!"

John smiled at the people's kindness. He was tired and had hoped to quietly slip away, but he wanted to acknowledge these simple and generous people. "Thank you! How could I refuse such a thoughtful invitation?"

In the morning, John celebrated Mass and blessed the people. Then he gathered his belongings and opened the door to leave. "Where's my sleigh?" he asked.

"Right there," said one of the priests, pointing to an elegant sleigh.

"But that's not the one I had just yesterday," replied John, with a look of shock on his face. "This one is far too fancy for a simple man such as me!"

"Sir," said a man who had descended from the magnificent sleigh, "Prince Schwarzenberg, a Bohemian nobleman, sent me. He insisted that his sleigh be available to take you to Prachatitz."

"You must ride home in style!" added one of the priests. "You are a bishop, a native son."

John looked at the beaming faces of the priests and townspeople. He saw the expectant look on everyone's faces and noticed the driver holding the reins ready. John didn't want to disappoint them, so he got in the sleigh. Then, raising his hand in blessing, he prayed, "May God's abundant blessing be upon all of you."

Just as had happened on the road to Nettolitz, the people of Prachatitz gathered along the road to welcome him. The church bells at St. James rang loudly. The village band played merrily, and the honor guards saluted John as he rode into Prachatitz.

"Stop the sleigh at St. James Church, please. I want to thank Jesus for my safe arrival home," John told the driver.

The sleigh came to a halt, and John's feet crunched in the snow. Many of the people followed John into the church. Once inside, John quickly dropped to his knees.

Thank you, Jesus, for bringing me safely home. I'm so grateful to be here. Be with the faithful who knelt by the side of the road for a blessing and with the prince who lent me his sleigh. Thank you for your goodness to me and for always providing for my needs.

John rose and turned to the crowd and said, "My good people, what an honor it is for me to be welcomed so warmly by you. I'm just a simple man from Prachatitz whom our Lord has greatly blessed. He has fulfilled my deep desire to serve his people in the United States. . . . And now he has brought me back home for a short visit. Let us praise and thank him always!"

John then turned and went out on the village street. "I will walk, not ride, to my father's house!" he called to the sleigh driver as he grabbed his bag.

How I've missed this, he thought as he looked around the familiar landscapes.

Nearing his childhood home, John spotted a gray-haired man who stood stooping slightly by the gate. *Papa! He's almost 80 years old now,* he realized at once. *And that woman next to him waving at me must be—*

"John!" the woman called loudly. "John, it's me, your little sister Louise!" She ran forward to embrace John. "I can hardly believe it's you. You're home at last!"

"It's so good to see you, Louise, and . . . everyone!" he said, choking a little on his words.

They walked arm in arm toward Papa Philip, who said nothing for several minutes. He just stood and looked lovingly at his son with tear-filled eyes. "My son, the bishop! Welcome home! If only your mother were here. . . ."

Hugging his father, John replied, "But Papa, she *is* here. You know she must be looking down on us at this very moment!"

"I can hardly believe it's you. You're home at last!"

"And Wenzel—how is he doing, John?" asked his father inquisitively.

"Well, Papa, he loves his life as a Redemptorist brother. He lives in Detroit now, far from Philadelphia. I wish I had more opportunity to spend time with him," said John.

John spent seven wonderful days with his family. Everyone celebrated and was so happy to have him home. But before they knew it, it was time for John to return to the United States.

Much was awaiting John in Philadelphia.

22

ALWAYS BE READY

John returned to Philadelphia and, for the next six years, worked to provide for the people of his diocese. He was always filled with zeal to do God's work, but his health was not good.

"Bishop Neumann, is something wrong? You don't look well," Father Sourin said with concern. He had come over to the bishop's residence for dinner and found John looking pale and tired.

"Edward, don't worry. I'm fine, just fine," John replied with a weak smile.

"No, you're not; you've been working too hard!" Father Sourin insisted.

"I do feel a *little* under the weather, but it will pass. Let's eat, I'm hungry!" said John. Then, trying to distract Father Sourin, he added, "I want to fill you in on what's been happening with the Franciscan sisters. Father Hespelein has been working with some women at St. Peter's parish. It looks like the little community is getting off to a good start!"

The next day, John woke up with a headache. *Why am I feeling so badly?* he wondered. *Maybe I should rest a little this afternoon. But first I must go down to my office and get a few things done.*

After sitting down at his desk, John heard a knock. He looked up at the person in the doorway, but he did not recognize the priest for a moment. *Who is this?* he wondered. Just then, John realized he knew the priest at his door very well; he was a fellow Redemptorist.

"Father Urbanczek, come in. It's good to see you," John said as he rose and extended his hand. "I remember our time together at St. Alphonsus in Baltimore." Then with a smile, John added, "How I miss all of my Redemptorist brothers!"

Father Urbanczek smiled, "You are needed here, Bishop Neumann." But then he added, "Bishop, you look sick; your eyes are glassy. Are you feeling well?"

"Not the best; I feel a bit strange today," replied John. "But I have some business to attend to with our lawyer this afternoon. I'm sure that the walk and fresh air will do me good."

"Well, do take care of yourself," the priest said with concern. Then, remembering why he had come, Father Urbanczek added, "Bishop, I stopped by to ask for your blessing on my parish mission. We begin tomorrow evening in New York."

"Those missions do much good for our people," John said. "Why don't you kneel for a moment and I'll ask for God's blessing."

Father Urbanczek knelt while John extended his hand.

"Come, Holy Spirit," John prayed, "descend on Father Urbanczek as he prepares to proclaim your Word tomorrow evening. I bless you in the name of the Father, and of the Son, and of the Holy Spirit."

Father Urbanczek rose to leave and John told him, "A man must always be ready. Death comes whenever and wherever our good God wills it."

That afternoon, John sat in the lawyer's office to sign some papers to buy a plot of land for another parish school. "I'm happy we will soon have another Catholic school in Philadelphia!" he said with delight. John signed the necessary papers with a shaky hand. "Now I must be off to the post office to see if a chalice I ordered has arrived. Have a good afternoon!" John said cheerfully.

On his way to the post office, John crossed Vine Street.

As he reached the curb, he staggered. A sharp pain shot through his head, and John fell to the ground, landing on the front steps of a home.

Several young men saw John fall and ran to help. The front door of a nearby house opened wide and a man looked out.

"Bring him in here," the kind man offered, opening the door wide. Two young men lifted John and carried him into the house.

"Who is this poor man?" the homeowner asked.

The two young men carefully laid John down on the rug in front of the lit fireplace. Opening his coat, they found his pectoral cross.

"It's the bishop!" said one of the men. "We must send a messenger at once to the bishop's residence on Logan Square!"

Father Carter, a priest of the diocese, arrived a short time later to anoint John, but he had already passed away. It was January 5, 1860, and John was forty-eight years old. The few possessions he had with him included some peppermint candy that he liked to give to children, and a simple worn rosary, which he often prayed with as he walked. His pocket also contained a piece of paper on which he had written: *Live each day as if it were your last.* Even though he died suddenly, he was certainly well prepared to meet God.

The news of John's sudden death spread quickly throughout the city. Telegraph wires spread the news to the far corners of his diocese. Coal miners, farmers, factory workers, school children, orphans, prisoners, the sick—everyone who had come to know the "Little Bishop" (as he was sometimes called) grieved his loss. He had been their friend. When his body was waked in the cathedral, thousands of the poor immigrants he had helped poured in to pay their respects.

Four days later, on January 9, the funeral procession wound through city streets starting from Logan Square to the Pro-Cathedral of St. John's. Crowds of people gazed on the wooden casket in the glass-walled, horse-drawn hearse as it passed by with John's body. Archbishop Kenrick of Baltimore gave the homily at the funeral Mass. The city had never seen such a public display of sorrow. Philadelphia's Little Bishop would be greatly missed.

Since John had expressed the wish to be buried among his Redemptorist brothers, his body was buried at the Redemptorist parish, Saint Peter's, at Fifth and Girard Avenue in Philadelphia.

Pope Paul VI beatified John Neumann on October 13, 1963. His canonization followed on June 19, 1977. He was the first North American bishop to be canonized.

The Church celebrates his feast day on January 5.

PRAYER

Saint John Neumann, you loved Jesus so much that you wanted to spend your life serving him. You left your family, your friends, and your country because you loved God and wanted to serve him as a missionary in the United States. Even though the way was difficult, you trusted that Jesus would always lead you and provide.

Help me to listen to Jesus so he can lead me, too. Help me to trust him always. Saint John, help me to be courageous in sharing my faith with others. Amen.

GLOSSARY

1. *Ad Limina* **visit**—an obligatory visit that bishops make at stated times to present themselves to the pope and to talk about what is happening in their dioceses.

2. **Bohemia**—now part of the Czech Republic, in John Neumann's lifetime this territory belonged to the Austrian Empire.

3. **Cassock**—an ankle-length robe sometimes worn by priests and religious brothers.

4. **Chalice**—a sacred cup, often plated with gold, used to hold the Blood of Christ in the celebration of the Eucharist.

5. **Diocese**—a part of the Church made up of Catholics within a certain geographical area.

6. **Dogma of the Immaculate Conception**—a defined teaching that means Mary was preserved from original sin from the moment of her conception and filled with grace. Mary received this unique privilege because she was to be the Mother of Jesus. Since Jesus is God and therefore all-holy,

it was right that Mary be preserved from sin. The Immaculate Conception was proclaimed a dogma in 1854. We celebrate the feast of the Immaculate Conception on December 8. It is a holy day of obligation in the United States.

7. **Episcopal motto**—motto or slogan of a bishop usually found on a coat of arms.

8. **Feast of Saint Wenceslaus**—popular autumn festival commemorating the death of the Bohemian prince.

9. **Habit (of a religious order)**—a uniform worn by some religious sisters, brothers, and priests to identify them as a member of a particular religious institute. A habit is a sign of their dedication to God and the Church.

10. **Infallible**—to be without error when teaching about faith or morals. The pope's teaching is infallible under certain, very specific conditions.

11. **Litany of the Saints**—a litany is a type of prayer composed of a list of names or titles followed by a response that is repeated many times. In the Litany of the Saints, after each saint's name is said, the response is "pray for us."

12. **Monstrance**—a vessel used to show the Eucharist for adoration. The monstrance is often decorated with precious stones or plated with gold or silver.

13. **Novice**—a person who enters a religious congregation of men or women and is preparing to profess vows of poverty, chastity, and obedience.

14. **Novitiate**—a period of time, now usually one or two years, in which novices who have responded to God's call to religious life prepare to make the vows through which they will totally offer their lives to Jesus.

15. **Ordination**—the action by which the sacrament of Holy Orders is conferred on a man.

16. **Pectoral cross**—a cross or crucifix worn on a long chain around the neck so that it rests on the chest; worn especially by bishops, abbots, and priests.

17. **Philosophy**—the study of the basic principles of life and the world through the use of reason.

18. **Prayer of consecration**—the prayer by which a person is set apart for religious service, for example the office of bishop.

19. **Providence of God**—God's care and concern for his creation: keeping it in existence and overseeing his loving and wise plan for it.

20. **Rectory**—parish house where the pastor and other priests live.

21. **Religious priest**—a priest who belongs to an order or community of men bound together by faith and the vows of poverty, chastity, and obedience.

22. **Redemptorists**—a group of missionary priests founded by Saint Alphonsus Maria Liguori in 1732 in Italy. Redemptorists are male religious who live in a community and keep the three vows of poverty, chastity, and obedience.

23. **Sacrament of the Sick**—a sacrament administered by a priest or bishop to those who are seriously ill, elderly, or in danger of death. Through the blessed oil of the sick and the words of this sacrament, God offers spiritual healing, the forgiveness of sin, strength to cope with the condition, peace, and sometimes physical healing. This sacrament was formerly called Extreme Unction.

24. **Seminary**—a place where men prepare to become priests by study and spiritual life.

25. **Spiritual Director**—a person who guides or directs another in the spiritual life.

26. **Surplice**—a loose, white vestment of half-length that is worn by clergy and sometimes laity who are serving in a liturgical ceremony.

27. **Stole**—a long, narrow cloth that bishops and priests wear around their necks and deacons wear over their left shoulders for liturgical celebrations.

28. **Tabernacle**—a fixed, locked box where the Blessed Sacrament is kept in churches or, with the permission of the local bishop, in a convent or rectory.

29. *Veprove se zelim*—a Bohemian dish made of pork with cabbage.

30. **Vocation**—the call of God for a person to become holy through a certain way of life, such as marriage, the priesthood, or the consecrated life. Everyone is called to holiness.

31. **Vow**—an important promise made freely to God. Members of religious communities usually make the vows of chastity, poverty, and obedience.

The Saints
Pray for Us

For over two thousand years holy men and women have followed Jesus with amazing dedication, courage, and creativity. This beautifully illustrated book guides you in asking the saints to pray for you!

The
SAINTS
Pray
for Us

Bible for
Young Catholics

Every book of the Old and
New Testaments comes to
life through the pages of this
book with colorful illustrations,
maps, and historical notes.

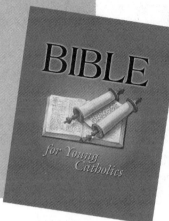

Prayers for
Young Catholics

This book of basic and more
advanced prayers, beautifully
expressed through interior
artwork, explains the importance
of prayer and provides instruction
on how to pray.

Who are the
Daughters of St. Paul?

We are Catholic sisters with a mission. Our task is to bring the love of Jesus to everyone like Saint Paul did. You can find us in over 50 countries. Our founder, Blessed James Alberione, showed us how to reach out to the world through the media. That's why we publish books, make movies and apps, record music, broadcast on radio, perform concerts, help people at our bookstores, visit parishes, host JClub book fairs, use social media and the Internet, and pray for all of you.

Visit our Web site at www.pauline.org

BOOKS & MEDIA

The Daughters of St. Paul operate book and media centers at the following addresses. Visit, call, or write the one nearest you today, or find us at www.paulinestore.org.

CALIFORNIA
3908 Sepulveda Blvd, Culver City, CA 90230   310-397-8676
3250 Middlefield Road, Menlo Park, CA 94025   650-369-4230

FLORIDA
145 S.W. 107th Avenue, Miami, FL 33174   305-559-6715

HAWAII
1143 Bishop Street, Honolulu, HI 96813   808-521-2731

ILLINOIS
172 North Michigan Avenue, Chicago, IL 60601   312-346-4228

LOUISIANA
4403 Veterans Memorial Blvd, Metairie, LA 70006   504-887-7631

MASSACHUSETTS
885 Providence Hwy, Dedham, MA 02026   781-326-5385

MISSOURI
9804 Watson Road, St. Louis, MO 63126   314-965-3512

NEW YORK
64 W. 38th Street, New York, NY 10018   212-754-1110

SOUTH CAROLINA
243 King Street, Charleston, SC 29401   843-577-0175

TEXAS
Currently no book center; for parish exhibits or outreach evangelization, contact: 210-569-0500, or SanAntonio@paulinemedia.com, or P.O. Box 761416, San Antonio, TX 78245

VIRGINIA
1025 King Street, Alexandria, VA 22314   703-549-3806

CANADA
3022 Dufferin Street, Toronto, ON M6B 3T5   416-781-9131

¡También somos su fuente para libros,
videos y música en español!